PATHS OF THE BEGGAR WOMAN

First published 2008 by
Worple Press
PO Box 328
Tonbridge
Kent TN9 1WR

Copyright © Belinda Cooke

The right of Belinda Cooke to be identified as the author of this work has been asserted by her in accordance with the Copyrights, Designs and Patents Act, 1988. All rights reserved.

British Library Cataloguing in Publication data.
A catalogue record for this book is available from the British Library

ISBN 978 1 905208 11 1

Worple Press is an independent publisher specialising in poetry, art and alternative titles. **Worple Press** can be contacted at:

Worple Press
PO Box 328
Tonbridge
Kent TN9 1WR

Tel: 01732 368958
E-mail: theworpleco@aol.com
Website: www.worplepress.co.uk

Typset and printed by Q3 Digital/Litho, Loughborough, Leicestershire

PATHS OF THE BEGGAR WOMAN

*THE SELECTED POEMS OF
MARINA TSVETAEVA*

TRANSLATED BY

Belinda Cooke

DEDICATION

For Richard

CONTENTS

ACKNOWLEDGEMENTS	9
INTRODUCTION	11

EVENING ALBUM
The Meeting	19
In Paris	20

POEMS OF YOUTH
You there, walking	23
For my poems, written so early	24
You who don't come near me	25
To Sergey Efron-Durnovo	26
Already how many have fallen into this abyss	27
To My Grandmother	29
A Woman Friend:	
Are you happy? Don't tell me. Hardly	30
That dream recalled from yesterday	31
Today the thaw set in	32
You were too lazy to dress	33
Today at seven the sleighs headed off	34
I am glad that you are not sick because of me	35
I did not keep The Commandments	36
Two suns are cooling – God forgive me	37
O gypsy passion for parting	38

VERSTS
No one has taken anything away	41
You throw back your head	42
Four years old	43
Poem about Moscow:	
Clouds all around	45
Take from my hands, my strange and beautiful brother	46
Squares hurry us past	47
The sad day will come they say	48
Thunderous bells echoed across	49

The bells rain down on the blue groves	50
The rowan tree blazed up	51
Insomnia:	
Dark circles about the eyes	52
I love to kiss	54
In my vast city it is night	55
After a sleepless night the body is weak	56
Now I am a heavenly guest	57
This night I am alone in the night	58
Insomnia my friend	59
Poems to Alexander Blok:	
Your name – a bird in the hand	61
Tender ghost	62
You walk to the west of the sun	64
For the animal – his lair	65
Where I live in Moscow – the cupolas burn	66
They thought he's just a man	67
I'm almost certain – beyond that grove	68
And clouds of gadflies buzz around oblivious nags	69
Here he is – look – risen from a strange land	70
Like a weak light through the darkness of hells	71
Poems to Akhmatova:	
Muse of lamentation, finest of muses	72
I stand here with my head in my hands	73
With one final sweeping movement	74
The name of the child is Lev	75
How many fellow travellers and friends	76
You'll stick close to me for I am your prisoner	77
You block out the sun at its height	78
My two hands have been given to me to reach out to everyone	79
White sun and the low, low clouds	80
If only fate had brought you and I together	81
The world's nomadic lands began in darkness	82
Dear companions, who've spent the night with us	83

UNCOLLECTED POEMS (1910-1916)

No doubt we'll meet in hell, my passionate sisters	87
In order to reach lips and the bed	88
I shall reclaim you from all lands, from all the heavens	89

PSYCHE
To Alya   93

UNCOLLECTED POEMS (1916-1921)
To Sonechka   97
    Some are created from stone, some are created from clay   98
    Yesterday he still looked me in the eyes   99

AFTER RUSSIA
There is an hour for these words   103
Unfaithful love   104
Earth Omens   105
Night-time whispers: a hand   106
Find yourself friends who are trusting   107
Remember the law   108
A time will come Lord   109
Ophelia to Hamlet   110
Ophelia in Defence of the Queen   111
Phaedra:
    The Complaint   112
    The Message   114
Eurydice to Orpheus   115
Poets:
    The poet - brings speech from far off   116
    In the world you'll find the superfluous…   117
    What shall I do, blind and a stepson   118
A Dialogue between Hamlet and his Conscience   119
Magdalene:
    Between us the Ten Commandments   120
    Ointments bought for three times their value   121
    I shall not torment you for what you do   122
An Attempt at Jealousy   123

UNCOLLECTED POEMS (1921-1941)
Longing for Home   127

Poems to Czechoslovakia
   To Germany   129
   They Took…   131
   What tears in our eyes now   132
It's time to remove the amber   133

NOTES   135

BIBLIOGRAPHY   140

ACKNOWLEDGEMENTS

Some of these translations have appeared in the following publications to whose editors grateful acknowledgement is made: *Acumen, Agenda, Chapman, Coffee House Poetry, Flaming Arrows, London Magazine, Magma, Monomyth, Poetry Ireland Review, Poetry Salzburg Review, Shearsman, South, The Shop, Stand* and *The Use of English*.

I am indebted to many of Marina Tsvetaeva's translators and researchers and have listed texts that have been helpful to me in my bibliography. A particular mention must be made of Elaine Feinstein's translations produced in collaboration with Angela Livingstone (and 'Poem of the End' with Valentina Coe). As the only available text in the seventies, it was an invaluable aid when I was trying to get to grips with Tsvetaeva's poetry in Russian as a student. I would like to thank Arnold McMillin, my professor at Liverpool – who first introduced me to Russian poetry, as well as the encouraging discussions with Gerry Smith who was a Reader there at the time.

Many people have looked over these translations with helpful suggestions: Alten and Albert Brenham, Kris Long and Peter Robinson. Joy Hendry's editing of my *Chapman* selection impacted on my work for the whole collection and her assistance in editing parts of the text was invaluable. Olga Sevastyanova had perceptive insights into many of Tsvetaeva's challenging poems in *After Russia*, and Olga Andreyev Carlisle, as well as discussing the poetry, has also always shown great kindness in sharing her personal memories of Silver Age poets she met as a child.

Richard McKane's name walks before him for his selfless commitment to Russian and Turkish poets and their translators. For the past ten years he has been an invaluable friend, always happy to discuss, collaborate, and second read my work, including this text. I shall be ever grateful and this volume is dedicated to him.

I would also like to thank my family for their support: David for sharing his poetry enthusiasm over the years, Paul for his willingness to burn the midnight oil and Brian, Martin and my mum for just being there. Finally, I must thank my husband Stephen whose continuing support and patience have left me free to pursue my various obsessions over the past twenty-five years.

INTRODUCTION

One Victim of War and Exile – the Fate of Marina Tsvetaeva

In Russia, apart from for the privileged few, the turn of the century was not a good time to be born. Fates were sealed by the relentless cataclysms of Russian history: revolution, civil war, Stalin's Purges and the final devastation of the Second World War – a war largely won by Stalin's willingness to see the lives of his own people as cheap, true to his belief that 'the death of a single person is a tragedy, the death of millions is a statistic'. Tsvetaeva's life *was* tragic, leading eventually to suicide, her personal tragedy inextricably interwoven with the harsh and momentous events taking place around her, yet, despite everything, she produced a more-than-remarkable body of poetry. Indeed, Joseph Brodsky has argued that Tsvetaeva is possibly the greatest poet of the twentieth century.

A woman of uncompromising temperament, it was inevitable that she would opt for exile rather than enduring life under the Bolshevik Soviet Union. During the Civil War she was separated from her husband, Sergey Efron, for five years, during which she suffered extreme poverty to the extent that her second daughter Irina died of malnutrition in an orphanage. During the thirties, while poets like Anna Akhmatova, Osip Mandelstam and Boris Pasternak were suffering from Stalin's repression, Tsvetaeva was living the freer life of the exile but as a result she was deprived of the recognition that all these other writers had from the Russian people.

Life gradually took on a more sinister turn. Driven by fierce nostalgia and naivety, many exiled Russians in Berlin, Paris and Prague were gradually enticed back to the Soviet Union and offered Soviet passports. Gradually, Tsvetaeva became isolated from her family as her daughter and son sided with Efron in wishing to return. They were unaware that many returning exiles would end up condemned to hard labour in Stalin's vast Gulag. For some there was an even worse outcome: Professor Mirsky of the University of London for example, was shot shortly after his return in the thirties.

Finally it came to light that her husband who had become increasingly involved with Soviet Russia had been spying for the Russians working for the NKVD (People's Commissariat for Internal Affairs). He was taken back to Russia after being implicated in the assassination of a Russian defector in Paris. Though most agree that Tsvetaeva was innocent of all this she was, from this point, ostracised by the émigré community and had little choice but to follow Efron in her own words 'like a dog'. Shortly after returning, Efron and her daughter were taken away – Efron, ultimately, to be shot and her daughter, to the Gulag. Left with just her son and petrified of the fast-approaching war the writing was on the wall for Tsvetaeva. Suffering extreme depression, she committed suicide in Elabuga. Irma Kudrova's *The Death of a Poet: the Last Days of Marina Tsvetaeva* tracks Tsvetaeva's last movements. Kudrova puts forwards various possible reasons for Tsvetaeva's suicide, the most controversial of which is the suggestion that she might have been put under pressure by the NKVD to act as an informer. Without more concrete evidence such theories cannot go beyond speculation, but what *is* certain is that Tsvetaeva had been contemplating suicide for some time and had expressed this openly to many.

With her death there was only her sixteen-year-old son Georgy left to live out the closing chapters of her story. Though some helped him, including Akhmatova and Pasternak, he was in essence completely alone. His diaries reflect a petrified young man having to cope with near-starvation and tormented by a fear of being found in Moscow without the right papers. Although he had aspirations to write and study he was to die two years after Tsvetaeva, also a marked man. Though there have been various contradictory stories about 'Mur', there now seems little doubt that, in order to 'make amends' for having a father who was 'an enemy of the people', he must have been conscripted into one of Stalin's infamous Punishment Battalions. These were the troops sent on ahead to draw the enemy fire, clear mines etc. resulting in a 90 percent death rate. NKVD troops were placed at the back to ensure that these soldiers 'did their duty'. So the son Tsvetaeva had adored and believed would be better without her set the final seal on her tragedy. Few would dispute that Russia won the war for the allies but this was achieved by means of a very simple tactic – it didn't matter how many Russians the Germans killed as they ploughed ever deeper into Russia, Stalin's people were, in the words of one historian, 'like ants, ever more would keep on coming'.

The title of this book is an attempt to show Tsvetaeva as just one of Stalin's many victims, as well as a woman driven by a single-minded pursuit of her poetic muse. The 'Beggar woman' draws attention both to her desperate poverty and literal need to beg at times and to the various hyperbolic female selves seen in the poetry – one moment sovereign or godlike: 'What's it like living with another woman now that your queen has come down from her throne?' to one who idolises: (of Blok) 'in your sacred name / I shall kiss the evening snow' or (of Akhmatova) 'after giving you my all / I move away like a beggar woman'. The various 'paths' this 'beggar woman' was forced to pursue lends even greater weight to her poetry.

She herself elaborates on this in a letter entitled *Our own Paths* to the editor of a Russian journal:

> What are our own paths? Paths that grow up beneath our feet and become overgrown in our wake, neither the highway of luxury nor the rumbling track of labour, but our own paths, pathless paths. Pathless! There – I've reached my favourite word.... I am pathless myself, all poets are pathless – they follow their own paths...a path is the only property of the 'pathless'! It is their only possibility of property – and, more generally, it is the only instance of any kind of property being sacred: the solitary paths of creative work...I am also captivated by the fact ... that there are many, many paths – just as there are many different people and many different passions!

Tsvetaeva acts as a particularly inspirational role model for women poets with families to bring up – something Elaine Feinstein noted when she first encountered her verse – due to her ability to pursue the divided paths of every day living – domesticity and childcare – and the path of the poet. One cannot fail to note the contrast with Pasternak's situation: he lived in a comfortable 'large dacha' with a wife who created an environment that allowed him to write; he even had a 'small dacha' and mistress close by to provide a convenient muse. Tsvetaeva's pursuit of her various poetic muses was necessarily a far more chaotic process which involved the crossing of numerous lovers' paths. Yet, had she enjoyed such calmness and stability one feels she might have had to transform it into a storm to allow the poetry out. Though she often bemoans the lack of peace to write in her everyday situation, domestic calm would have been anathema to her writing – life needed to be lived on the edge if she was to be inspired to write.

Tsvetaeva writes powerfully and prolifically in a highly original style. It is difficult to convey the gutsiness of her harsh masculine rhymes and use of monosyllables, though one can get some sense of a defiant hyperbole that conceals an inner vulnerability. In tone, some of her poetry has affinities with Sylvia Plath's, as in say, 'Daddy', 'The Applicant' or 'Lady Lazarus'. Ultimately, though, her voice is like no one else's. Her poetry reflects a desire to devour life: 'I will sin – as I sin – as I sinned: with passion/ The Lord has given me senses – all five'. Every emotion is on a knife-edge, whether it be for a person or a locale. This is seen in her early poems, where we find a young woman who doesn't quite understand why she is driven by such strong feelings and this unrestrained passion continues throughout her life. Even in poems devoted to literary or biblical characters her sympathy lie with those unable to control their emotions – Phaedra, Gertrude or Mary Magdalene.

Tsvetaeva needed to have an object to project her emotions onto in order to function as a poet. One outcome of this was an intense, possessive, at times even claustrophobic obsession with the loved one. Such passion may be a reflection of intense admiration for a poet or of romantic love. She had numerous love affairs throughout her life, both during the Efron's absence and when they were together. In the early days, this caused him a lot of heartache. Her very open affair with the poet Sophia Parnok, for example, was a devastating blow to him. In her sequence to Moscow, she combines her love of this city with her passion for Osip Mandelstam with whom she also had a brief affair – which produced several poems on both sides. With time, Efron came to accept these affairs as part of her makeup and would conveniently remove himself till the heat died down. Often, indeed, these affairs tend to be in absentia, with the object of the passion almost irrelevant to the power of the emotion. Such lovers were all grist to the mill to her in producing her poetry. The most intriguing was the three-way relationship between herself, Pasternak and Rilke. The passionate letters that passed between them show Rilke and Pasternak as soulmates similarly able to inhabit these dual worlds of poetry and everyday life. That Tsvetaeva never actually met Rilke and that her real life encounters with Pasternak were always problematic (though they corresponded throughout their lives) reinforces the view that the resulting poetry has more substance than her many ephemeral relationships. Thus we have clear evidence of her divided paths: survival, family, the permanence of her marriage to Efron one sacrosanct path: the muse of ever-changing lovers to fuel her poetry another.

Yet, this said, it is perhaps the combination of literary and lovers' ties that left Pasternak feeling the greatest guilt at Tsvetaeva's suicide, after failing to provide her with the help she needed in her last days. In this context it should also not be forgotten that Tsvetaeva was notoriously difficult to deal with: though forced to beg help from others this did not prevent her maintaining the role of prima donna – for Tsvetaeva always knew her poetic worth in the eyes of fellow Russians. Olga Carlisle captured the essence of this paradox when she told me the tale of one of Olga's uncles who challenged someone to a duel for daring to be scathing about Tsvetaeva's poetry. Pasternak, whose domestic situation and political role made it difficult to accommodate Tsvetaeva at the time, never forgave himself, but he did all he could to help her children after her death. The haunting tone of the poem he dedicated to her provides the most fitting last word on this tragic victim of the twentieth century:

> Frowning, the dull day drags on.
> The rain streams inconsolably
> over the porch and entrance
> and into my open windows.
>
> Beyond the fence along the road
> the public garden is flooded.
> Clouds lie in disorder
> like beasts slumped in their lair.
>
> With the weather so overcast
> the book haunts me with thoughts
> of the earth and her beauty.
> I draw you a pine cone on the title page.
>
> Ah Marina, surely it's time now,
> and it's really no trouble for us
> to carry your abandoned ashes
> in requiem from Elabuga.

Over the past year I have been thinking
of how you would be transported solemnly
over the snows of the empty stretch of river
where the long boats winter on the ice.

It's so difficult for me since that time
to imagine you dying
like a miserly millionairess
among your starving sisters.

What shall I do to please you?
Somehow let me know.
In the silence of your departure
there is an unspoken reproach.

Losses are always puzzling.
I struggle to no purpose
in my futile attempts to find an answer.
Death leaves no tracks.

Here there are only half words and shadows,
slips of the tongue and self-deception,
and only faith in resurrection
provides some kind of point.

Winter is like luxurious funeral feasts:
stealthily I leave the house
to add to the twilight currents,
to spill wine down onto the Kasha.

Apple trees and snowdrifts before the house,
the town in a snowy shroud,
your enormous epitaph
seemed to me as the whole year.

Turning one's face to God
you drag yourself towards him from the earth,
as in those earlier days when here
on earth life just did not add up.

EVENING ALBUM

THE MEETING

Evening smoke rose over the town, while somewhere
into the distance carriages dutifully headed off.
Suddenly it flashed past – transparent anemone –
there in the window the face of one still just a child.

Eyelids in shadow. Curls lay about
in the likeness of a crown...I held back a cry:
I realised in this short moment
how our groans wake the dead.

That girl at the dark window,
vision of paradise in the station chaos,
how often I have met her in the valleys of sleep.

But why was she sad, this transparent silhouette?
Why was she searching restlessly? Perhaps for her
even in heaven there is no happiness?...

IN PARIS

Houses to the stars and sky below,
so close to the intoxicated earth.
In Paris, so immense and full of life,
there is always the same secret longing.

The noise of evening boulevards,
sunset's final fading ray...everywhere,
everywhere endlessly, couples, couples:
quivering lips and flirtatious looks.

I am alone here. How sweet it is to rest
my head against this horse chestnut.
In my heart weep lines from Rostand,
as they did in my abandoned Moscow.

Paris at night is alien and pitiful to me,
my heart still full of some earlier passion:
I walk home...to the sadness of violets
and someone's fond portrait.

There I'll find a sad, brotherly gaze,
a tender profile on the wall...
Rostand, the tormented Reichstadt
and Sarah will all come to me in sleep.

In Paris, so immense and full of life,
I dream of grass and clouds, and further off
laughter, while shadows are close by
and pain as before is deep.

POEMS OF YOUTH

You there, walking
with your eyes downcast
as mine once were:
pause here for a moment.

With your bunch of poppies
and buttercups, you will read
that my name was Marina,
and how old I was.

Don't think: here is a grave,
that I shall rise up to threaten you…
I myself loved to laugh
too much when I shouldn't.

My face all flushed
beneath a flood of curls…
I also existed, just like you
so just pause here for a moment.

Pluck the wild stalk
and the fruit with it, you'll find
nothing larger or sweeter than
wild strawberries from the cemetery.

Only don't stand sullenly
your head down on your chest.
Think about me easily.
Forget about me easily…

How you will glow in the light,
surrounded in golden dust…
So don't let my voice startle you
as it sounds from below the earth.

For my poems, written so early,
that I didn't know I was a poet,
bursting forth like water from a fountain,
like sparks from a rocket.

Like little devils broken loose
into the sleep and incense of a sanctuary,
for my poems of youth and death,
my unread poems!

Collecting dust at the back of shops
(where no one's going to buy them),
my poems mature like vintage wine —
I know their time will come.

You who don't come near me,
but avoid my dubious charms,
if only you knew how much fire,
how much life is squandered for nothing,

and how much heroic passion
there is in each chance shadow or sound,
how powder wasted all for nothing
reduced my heart to ashes.

O trains flying in the night
carrying a dream at the station…
But, I know, even if you could have,
you would not have recognised then

why my speech is so abrupt
in the endless smoke of my cigarette,
how much dark and menacing longing
is in my light-haired head.

TO SERGEY EFRON-DURNOVO

Certain voices instil only
silence in the listener,
so one predicts miracles.
He has such enormous eyes
the colour of the sea.

Take a good look at him —
his forehead and brows
and compare him with yourself.
That pale blue weariness
of ancient blood.

Blueness triumphs
in each noble vein.
He gestures like a tsarevich
or lion — endless lace,
like white foam.

Your regiment is the dragoons:
Decembrists and Men of Versailles.
And, being so young, one cannot know
whether his fingers will ask
for brushes, swords or strings.

Already how many have fallen into this abyss,
yawning out in the distance.
The day will come when I too will disappear
from the face of the earth.

Everything that sang and fought
and shone out will become frozen:
my green eyes, and my tender voice,
and golden hair.

And life with its daily bread will
become part of day's forgetfulness.
And everything will be as though beneath the sky
I had never existed.

Just like children who are changeable
and wicked for a short while,
that precious hour when the wood in the fire
turns to ash...the sounds of

the cello, the procession in the forest depths,
the bell in the village...
me so alive and real
on the tender earth.

To all of you I say, what's it to me
whether you are friends or strangers?
I turn to you demanding trust,
pleading for love.

Day and night, for words spoken
and written, the truth, for *yes* and *no*
because I am so often too sad
and only twenty years old...

Because I am bound to ask
you to forgive the offence,
because of my unrestrained affection
and arrogant air,

because of the speed of streaming events,
because of the truth, because of the game.
Listen. Just love me
because I will die.

TO MY GRANDMOTHER

The severe oblong oval
of your black bell-shaped dress...
young grandmother, who kissed
your haughty lips?

Hands which in the palace halls
played Chopin waltzes...
along your icy face
ran spiral-shaped curls.

Dark, straight and exacting glance,
a look ready to defend itself.
Young women never look like that.
Young grandmother, who are you?

How many possibilities, and how many
impossibilities, did you carry away
into the insatiable, gluttonous earth,
twenty year old Polish girl?

The day was virginal and the wind was fresh,
the dark stars went out. Grandmother,
this cruel rebelliousness in my heart –
has it come from you?

A WOMAN FRIEND

1

Are you happy? Don't tell me. Hardly.
And it's better so.
It seems you have kissed too much,
hence your sadness.

All the heroines of Shakespearean tragedy
I see in you.
Such a tragic young lady –
no one saved you.

You have become so tired of love's
recitations.
An iron hoop in your bloodless hand –
so eloquent.

I love you. Sin lies above you
like some great storm cloud
because you are caustic and fiery
and best of all,

because our lives are so different
in the darkness of the roads,
because of your inspired temptations
and dark fate,

because you are my stern-browed demon,
I ask for your forgiveness,
because, even if you leapt out of your grave –
you can be sure they won't save you.

For this trembling, for the fact that perhaps
I am dreaming all this.
For this ironic fineness,
and for the fact that you are not him.

2

That dream recalled from yesterday
under the rug's luxurious caress...
What was it? Whose victory?
Who was defeated?

I think all of it over again,
suffering everything once more.
This thing which I have no word for,
could it be love?

Who was the hunter? Who the hunted?
What the devil has happened here?
What have you discovered, endlessly
purring there, my Siberian cat?

In that duel of strong wills
who was the ball, in whose hands?
Was it my heart or yours,
that flew at a gallop?

But what on earth was it?
What is there to feel sorry about?
I really couldn't say: Was I the victor?
Was I defeated?

3

Today the thaw set in, today
I stood at the window.
Sober glance, breast free,
calm once more.

I don't know why. Perhaps
the soul was simply tired,
and just didn't want to touch
the restless pencil.

So I just stood there in the mist
miles away from good and evil,
quietly drumming with a finger
along the faintly ringing glass.

With a soul no better or worse
than this very first encounter –
the mother-of-pearl pools,
where the firmament splashed,

the bird that flies past
and the dog that simply runs along,
and even the impoverished singer
did not bring me to tears.

Dear art of oblivion
with a soul already mastered.
Some great feeling
today melted in the soul.

4

You were too lazy to dress,
and too lazy to get up from the sofa.
But each of your future days
would be happy with my happiness.

You particularly dislike
walking late in the night and cold.
But each of your future hours
would be young with my happiness.

You did this without malice.
innocently and irreparably.
I was your youth,
which is passing by.

5

Today at seven, the sleighs headed off,
headlong like a bullet or a snowball
along the Bolshoi Lubianka,
off who knows where.

Already laughter rang out...
my expression hardened:
hair a reddish fur
and someone tall close by.

You were already with someone else,
with her you cleared the sleigh-road,
someone you cared for more,
and desired more than I.

'Oh je n'en plus, j'etouffe!'
you shouted at the top of your voice,
as your strong hand wrapped the
fur sleigh rug around her.

The world joyful and the evening intrepid
goods flew from your muff...
You rushed along into the snowy whirlwind,
gaze to gaze, fur coats entwined.

And it was the most cruel rebellion,
and the snow fell so white.
I gave you no more than
two seconds glance.

And I felt no anger as I ironed
my fur coat's long fleece.
O Snow Queen
your little Kay has frozen

I am glad, that you are not sick because of me,
and that I am not sick because of you,
that the heavy earthly ball will never
slip away beneath our feet. I am glad
that we can joke around, can be relaxed
and not play around with words,
and that we don't go red with embarrassment
if we so much as touch each other's sleeve.

I am glad also that before me
you can comfortably embrace another,
that you do not want me to burn
in hell's flames because I do not kiss you.
I am glad you don't call out my name, my dear,
night and day – in vain –
that there in the church silence
they will never sing alleluia over us.

I shall always be grateful that you,
unknowingly, love me thus:
for my night-time peace,
for the rarity of our sunset meetings,
for not walking with me beneath the moon,
for the sun which is not above our heads,
for the sad fact that you are not sick because of me,
and I am not sick because of you.

I did not keep the commandments, did not take the sacrament.
I will sin — as I sin — as I sinned: with passion
until they sing the liturgy over me.
The Lord has given me senses — all five.

Friends. Allies. You have set things on fire.
You, partners in crime — you, young teachers:
young men and women, trees, constellations, clouds —
To God at the Last Judgement we reply together — the Earth!

Two suns are cooling – God forgive me,
one in the sky, the other in my breast.

How these suns – can I forgive myself?
How these suns drove me to madness!

And both are cooling – they no longer cause me pain.
And the more powerful one is the first to cool.

O gypsy passion for parting.
You've only just met – and you break it off!
I put my head in my hands
and think, gazing into the night:

digging into our letters
no one has really grasped
the nature of our treachery –
the fact that we are faithful only to ourselves.

VERSTS

No one has taken anything away,
I am delighted that we are apart.
I kiss you across the
hundreds of miles that divide us.

I know our gift is unequal
my voice for the first time is silent.
Young Derzhavin, what can
my ill-bred verses signify to you?

I bless you on your fearful journey:
Fly young eagle.
You managed to look directly at the sun,
was my youthful gaze too intense?

No one gazed after you
with a more tender or irrevocable look…
I kiss you across the
hundreds of years that divide us.

You throw back your head
because you are proud and full of talk.
This February has led me to
a lively travelling companion.

Rattling our Ukrainian gold
and slowly exhaling smoke,
as solemn strangers
we walk about my native city.

I do not ask what hands carefully touched
your eyelashes, my beautiful one,
or when, and how, and with
whom, and how many times

your lips were kissed. My hungry spirit
has subdued that dream.
I honour that part of you which is
a god-like *ten-year old* boy.

Come, let's amble along the river
that washes the streetlamps' coloured beads.
Let's linger in the square where
young tsars have been seen.

Whistle out your childish pain
and hold your heart in the palm of your hand…
my composed and agitated
emancipated slave, farewell!

Four years old.
Eyes like ice.
Brows already lethal.
Today for the first time
from the Kremlin heights
you observe
the floating ice.

Blocks of ice, blocks of ice
and domes.
Golden ringing.
Silver ringing.
Arms folded,
mouth silent
with a deep frown like Napoleon
you contemplate – the Kremlin.

Mama, where does the ice go?
Forwards *golubka* –
past palaces, churches, gates,
forwards *golubka*.
The blue-eyed
gaze is anxious.
Do you love me, Marina?
Very much.
Forever?
Yes.

Quickly comes the sunset.
Quickly we go back:
you to your nursery
me, biting my lip, to
some letters – better left
unwritten.

But the ice
still
moves on.

POEMS ABOUT MOSCOW

1

Clouds – all around.
Domes – all around.
Over the whole of Moscow
how many hands were needed!
I elevate you, best of burdens,
my little imponderable
sapling.

In this marvellous city
in this peaceful city
where it seems to me
even in death I will be happy,
take this wreath
for you must reign, as well as grieve
o my first born.

Do not blacken your brows
when you fast during Lent,
but come out and honour all forty
of the forty churches.
Come on foot, with youthful steps:
everything is spacious
with its seven hills.

The time will come
when you too, tenderly
and bitterly, must
hand over Moscow
to your daughter.
As for me it's the freedom to dream,
the ringing sound:
Vagankova
early dawns.

2

Take from my hands, my strange and beautiful brother,
this city, not built by human hands.

Every one of its churches – forty times forty –
and the pigeons soaring over them.

And the *Spassky Gates* with its flowers,
where the Orthodox remove their hats,

starstudded chapel, refuge from evil,
where the floor, is threadbare from kisses.

Take from me, my ancient, inspired friend,
this incomparable circle of five cathedrals.

I shall lead my foreign guest there in the garden
into the chapel of *Unexpected Delights*.

The golden domes will shine
while the sleepless bells ring out.

And down from the crimson clouds
The Virgin Mary will shroud you in her cloak.

And you will rise, full of marvellous strength…
You will never deny, that you loved me.

3

Squares hurry us past
the night-time towers.
O, how terrible in the night
are the cries of young soldiers!

O, the loudness of your heart
this beast-like roaring.
Kiss me with passion, my love,
daring young blood.

With this dryness in my throat
what is the point in appearing holy?
In the chapel the *Iverskaya* icon burns
like a little golden coffer.

Let's put a stop to all this
now and light a candle,
so that what's on my mind
about you doesn't happen.

4

The sad day will come, they say,
when my eyes will no longer reign burn, or weep.
Cooled by alien coins they dart about like a flame.
And – like a twin having groped for his twin –
the sacred face will shine through the easy features.
O, finally I recognise you
with your fine elegant waist.

But from the distance, do I also see you?
A pilgrimage, bewildered, making
the sign of the cross along the black road:
it reaches out to my hand, which I did not
jerk back, and they no longer reject,
to my hand, which exists no more.

For the first time I do not respond
to your kisses, you who are living.
I am dressed from head to toe
in my finest clothes.
Nothing any longer causes me to blush,
for today it is my Holy Easter.

Along the streets of abandoned Moscow
I shall travel and you shall plod your way.
And no one will lag behind on the road,
and the first clod will fall on the coffin lid
and at last it will be permitted,
a selfish, lonely dream.
And nothing will be needed from now on
by the newly crowned boyar's wife – Marina.

5

Thunderous bells echoed across
the city rejected by Peter.

The roaring surf toppled
over the woman spurned by you.

Praise to Tsar Peter and to you o tsar!
But higher than all you tsars are the bells.

While they resound from the blue,
Moscow indisputably holds first place,

and all forty of the forty churches
laugh at the pride of the tsars!

6

The bells rain down on the blue groves
of the Moscow suburbs: blind men drag
themselves along the road to *Kaluga*.

This singing, perfect, Kaluga road, washes
away and washes away the names of humble strangers,
singing of God in the darkness.

And I think: some day, having wearied
of you my enemies and you my friends,
and even of the compliance of Russian speech,

I shall wear a silver cross on my breast.
I shall make the sign of the cross — and quietly set off along the path
along the old road to *Kaluga*.

7

The rowan tree blazed up
in red clusters.
Leaves were falling.
I was born.

There was the argument
of a hundred bells.
The day was Saturday:
St John the Divine.

Since then I have
always wanted to devour
the bitter cluster
of the fiery rowan tree.

INSOMNIA

1

Dark circles about the eyes —
Insomnia. Wreathe of darkness
crowning the eyes — insomnia.

Now you understand,
don't pray to idols in the night:
you are the idol worshipper
whose secret I betrayed.

There's little about you
that belongs to the day's sunlight.

You pale-faced one
take my pair of rings.
You croaked and brought disaster
down upon the shadowy crown.

Why is it you hardly ever called out to me?
Why is it you hardly ever slept with me?

You go to bed with a relaxed face.
People worship you.
I, insomnia,
will recite for you:

sleep, you who are so peaceful,
sleep, you who are so worthy,
sleep, woman
under the crown.

In order that you sleep more easily
I will be your singer.

Sleep little friend
restless one,
sleep, little pearl
sleep you who are so in need of sleep.

And for anyone we didn't write letters to
and for anyone we didn't make promises to…
sleep yourself.

And now the inseparable
are separated
and now your little hands
are no longer gripped.

Now you have stopped torturing yourself,
dear martyr.

Sleep is sacred.
Everyone sleeps.
The crown is removed.

2

I love to kiss
hands and I love
to name
and even more —
to open doors
wide open in the dark night!

Having listened close
to the heavy step
somewhere fading away,
how the wind rocks
the sleepy, sleepless forest.

Ah night!
Somewhere springs are flowing...
drowsiness...
I almost sleep.
Somewhere in the night
a man will drown.

3

In my vast city it is night
as I set out from my house of sleep.
And people think: a daughter, a wife,
but my thought only is: it is night.

The July wind marks my path.
Through some window the music's faint.
A violent wind blows till dawn,
tears right through you into the heart.

A black poplar and a light in the window.
A ringing on the tower – in the hand a flower.
The sound of a footstep but no one's there.
The sight of a shadow – but I'm not here.

Lights like threads of golden beads.
Taste of a night leaf, small in the mouth.
Free yourself of daily ties.
Realise friends – you dream of me.

4

After a sleepless night the body is weak,
endearing, no one's.— not your own.
Shooting pains run through your sluggish veins
and you smile at people, like a seraph.

After a sleepless night your hands are weak,
and friend or enemy it's all the same.
There is a whole rainbow in each chance sound
and a sudden scent of Florence rises from the frost.

Gradually colour comes to the lips, and shadow
lightens to gold around the sunken eyes.
It's the night that has set this most bright face on fire
and night's darkness remains only in our eyes.

5

Now I am a heavenly guest
in your country.
I saw the sleeplessness of the forest
and the sleep of the fields.

Somewhere in the night
horseshoes churned up the grass.
The cow breathed heavily
in the sleepy cowshed.

I'll tell you sadly
with all tenderness
about the goose-watchman
and the sleeping geese.

Hands plunged into dog fur.
The dog was grey.
Then towards six
dawn began.

6

This night I am alone in the night
a sleepless, homeless nun.
This night I have all the keys
to this, our unique capital.

Sleeplessness has pushed me along the path.
How fine you are, my dim Kremlin.
This night I kiss you on the breast,
this whole great howling earth!

This is not hair, but fur standing on end
and the choking wind blows straight into the soul.
This night I pity everyone:
those who are pitied and those who are kissed.

7

Insomnia my friend
again I meet you
offering the lasting cup
in the soundless
ringing night.

Enjoy it.
Take a sip.
Don't just *drink* it
knock it back.
I'll show you...
Such tender lips.
Dear one. Friend.
Take a sip.
Enjoy it.
Drink up.
Stand firm
before all passions –
Stay calm
from all you hear –
Friend.
Do me the honour.
Open your lips.
Take it from the cut glass cup
with the sweet bliss of your lips.
Take it.
Take it in.
Swallow it down.
Become no one.
O friend don't take it wrong.
Enjoy it.
Drink up.
The most passionate
of all passions – the most tender
of all deaths – from the two palms
of my hands – enjoy it – drink up.

The world has gone missing. Into nowhere —
flooded shores...
Drink *lastochka moia*. At the bottom
there are shining pearls...

You drink the sea.
You drink the sunset.
I ask you, child, what lover
could compare with
such a spree as this?

But if they ask (I will tell you what to say) —
Tell them that my cheeks looked pale, and how
I'm out on a spree with insomnia.
I'm out on a spree with insomnia...

POEMS TO ALEXANDER BLOK

1

Your name – a bird in the hand.
Your name – an ice cube on the tongue.
One single movement of the lips.
Your name is four letters,
a ball caught in flight,
a silver bell in the mouth.

A stone thrown in a quiet pond.
A sob like the sound of your name.
In the light tapping of night time hooves
your loud name thunders.
We name him with a loud clicking
Of a gun held to the temple.

Your name – it's impossible!
Your name – a kiss on the eyes,
in the tender hard frost of frozen eyelids.
Your name – a kiss in the snow.
A mouthful from a pale blue icy spring.
With the sound of your name comes a deep dream.

2

Tender ghost,
knight without reproach,
who called you
into my young life?

In the gloom – dove-coloured
you stand, dressed
in a chasuble of snow.

So that it is not the wind
that drives me through the town
for this is the third evening
I have sensed my enemy.

Snowy singer
you bewitched me
with your pale-blue eyes.

The snowy swan
spreads his feathers beneath my feet.
The feathers soar
and slowly sink onto the snow.

Thus, on feathers
I walk to the door,
beyond which – is death.

He sings to me
beyond the blue windows,
he sings to me
along with the distant sleigh bells,

With a shout that carries
like the swan's cry
he calls.

Dear ghost,
I know I am dreaming all this.
Be kind to me:
amen, amen.
Be generous – Amen.

3

You walk to the west of the sun.
You will see the evening light.
You walk to the west of the sun,
and the snowstorm covers your tracks.

Past my windows – passionless –
you will pass in the snowy silence,
my fine righteous man of God,
you are the soft light of my soul.

I do not hanker after your soul.
Your path is inviolable.
In a hand pale from kissing,
I shall not drive in a nail.

And I shall not call you by name.
And I shall not reach out my hands to you.
Before your sacred waxen face
I shall only worship from a distance.

And standing beneath the slowly falling snow
I shall sink down on my knees in the snow,
and in your sacred name
I shall kiss the evening snow –

there, where with a majestic tread
you walked past in funereal silence,
o soft light – sacred glory –
the almighty of my soul.

4

For the animal – his lair.
For the stranger – the road.
For the dead – the hearse.
To each – his own.

For the woman – to be cunning.
For the tsar – to rule.
For me – to praise
Your name.

5

Where I live in Moscow – the cupolas burn.
Where I live in Moscow – the bells ring.
Where I live the graves stand in rows,
in them the tsarinas and tsars are sleeping.

And don't you know, that at dawn it is easier
to breathe in the Kremlin than anywhere in all the earth.
And don't you know, that in the Kremlin at dawn
I will pray to you till sunset.

And you are passing over your Neva
at that time, as over the river Moskva
I stand with a bowed head, there where
the streetlamps cling together.

With all sleeplessness I love you.
With all sleeplessness I listen for you,
at that time when in the whole of the Kremlin
the bell ringers wake to ring the bells.

But my river – with your river,
but my hand – with your hand,
they will not join, my love, until
the dawn catches up with the sunset.

6

They thought he's just a man,
so they forced him to die.
Now he is dead forever.
Weep over the dead angel.

At sunset he sang
of the evening's beauty,
to the hypocritical flickering
of three wax flames.

Rays flowed from him,
glowing streamers across the snow.
Three wax candles,
to the sun, bearer of the light!

See how his dark eyelids
have fallen.
See how
his wings are broken.

The reader in black recites,
as lazy hands cross themselves...
The singer lies dead
and celebrates resurrection.

7

I'm almost certain — beyond that grove
is the village where I lived.
I'm almost certain — love is simpler
and easier than I thought.

You useless nags get moving!
A lifting and lashing of the whip,
and after the cry again the lash —
and once more the harness bells sing out.

Over the wretched swaying corn
one pole follows another,
and the wire beneath the sky
sings and sings of death.

8

And clouds of gadflies buzz around the oblivious nags,
and the native Kaluga calico is buffeted by the wind,
and the whistling of the quails, and the immense sky,
and bells resounding over the waves of corn,
and talk of Germans, until you've had it up to here,
and yellow…yellow, beyond the blue grove, a cross,
and sweet warmth and such a glow over everything,
and your name, sounding like: angel.

9

Here he is – look – tired of strange lands,
a leader without followers.

See how he cups his hands to drink from a swift mountain stream,
a prince without a country.

There he has everything he needs: principality
army, bread, and mother.

Rule your fine heritage:
friend without friends.

10

Like a weak light through the darkness of hells
your voice is heard through the roar of bursting shells.

And like some seraph in the midst of these storms
out from those ancient misty mornings

in a voice which is toneless, he tells us
the blind masses how much he loved us:

for the blue cloak, for the sin of treachery
and how the woman he loved most was the one who

plunged deepest into the night in pursuit of evil
and how he did not fall out of love with you, Russia.

And, moving a bewildered finger back
and forth across his temple, he goes on to tell

of such days as await us, how God will deceive us
how you will come to call the sun and – and it will not rise....

This is how, like the prisoner alone with himself
or, perhaps, a child speaking in their sleep,

we were presented – along all the wide squares –
with the sacred heart of Alexander Blok.

POEMS TO AKHMATOVA

1

Muse of lamentation, finest of muses,
you crazy offspring of the white night.
You inflict a black storm on Rus
and the arrows of your cries pierce us

and deafen us: we shy away, yet still a hundred
thousand times we swear an oath to you Anna
Akhmatova, this name, one enormous sigh,
tumbling into the nameless depths.

We have only been crowned because we walk
the same earth that you walk, walk beneath the same sky.
And he who has been wounded with your deathly fate
already descends to his deathbed immortal.

My city resounds. The domes shine.
The blind beggar praises the bright Saviour.
I give you my city of bells, Akhmatova,
and my heart into the bargain.

2

I stand here with my head in my hands —
so much for human intrigues.
I put my head in my hands and sing
at the late sunset.

Now I am lifted up on
the violent crest of a wave
I sing to you, who stand
a solitary moon, among us.

You flew down hook-nosed onto
my heart like a raven. You plunged
into the clouds. Your anger is deadly,
deadly, as your kindness.

You have spread your night
over my pure gold Kremlin.
The pleasure of your song
is a belt tight about my throat.

I am so happy. Never did
the sunset burn with such purity.
After giving you my all I
move away like a beggar woman.

Your voice, its depth its shadows,
has left me breathless. I am happy
to be the first to name you:
the Muse of Tsarskoe Selo.

3

With one final sweeping
movement her eyelashes close.
O this dear body. Dust
of this lightest of birds.

What did she do in the mist of days?
She waited and sang...
How great a sigh seemed to come
from such a little body.

Such sweet somnolence
beyond all human imagining...
In her there was something
of the angel and the eagle.

And she sleeps, and the choir
beckons her into the Garden of Eden,
as if the demon who has fallen asleep
has not had his fill of songs.

****

Hours, years, centuries neither we
nor our surroundings remain.
And the memorial placed there
no longer remembers.

For a long time the broom has been idle,
and over the Muse of Tsarskoe Selo
crosses of nettles
bow down in adulation.

4

The name of the child is Lev.
That of the mother is Anna.
In his name there is anger,
in his mother's silence.
His hair is red —
red tulip head!
Well then, Hosanna
to the little tsar.

God give him breath,
the smile of his mother,
and the vision of a pearl diver.
God, keep a careful eye on him,
the tsar's son, a fortune-teller
among the remaining sons.

Red-haired lion cub
with your green eyes,
a terrible legacy awaits you.

The oceans north and south,
the pearls of black rosary beads
lie in your cupped hands.

5

How many fellow travellers and friends —
you will play second fiddle to no one.
Pride and bitterness
rule such a tender youth.

Remember that stormy day in the port,
the roar of the Caspian,
the menace of southern winds
and some rose petal in your mouth.

How the gypsy woman gave you
a stone in a gilt frame,
how the gypsy woman told you some lies
something about fame...

And, high up in the sails,
a lad in his blue work clothes.
the thunder of the sea and the menacing call
of the wounded Muse.

6

You'll stick close to me for I am your prisoner
and you are my escort, we share the same fate,
and alone in the vacant emptiness
we have been given an order for fresh horses.

Look, I'm really quite calm.
I'm not hiding anything.
Won't you, guard, just let me
take a walk to that pine?

7

You block out the sun at its height,
all the stars in the palm of your hand.
Ah, if only – doors wide open –
I could bite into you like the wind!

If only I could prattle on, then turn red
and suddenly look away from you,
become subdued and softly whimper,
like the child who has been forgiven.

My two hands have been given to me to reach out to everyone
holding neither back, lips – to name,
eyes – not to see, their brows sweeping over them
tenderly to marvel at love and more tenderly at hate.

But that bell there heavier than the Kremlin's
unceasingly pounds and pounds in my breast –
who knows what it is? I don't. Perhaps it means
I won't get the chance to be a guest too long on the Russian earth.

White sun and the low, low clouds,
along the kitchen gardens, beyond the white wall, a graveyard.
And on the sand a line of straw scarecrows
under the crossbeams, the height of a man.

And having leaned over the picket fence
I see roads, trees, soldiers, at random. The old peasant woman
stands at the wicker gate, chewing and chewing
a black hunk of bread, heavily sprinkled with salt.

What angers you about these grey huts,
Lord — and why did you shoot so many through the chest?
The train passed and began to howl, and the soldiers raised a howl
and in its wake it made dust, and more dust...

No, to die. Better never to have been born,
than this sorrowful, pitiful convict howling
for these black-browed beautiful women. O and now
the soldiers are singing. O my Lord God.

If only fate had brought you and I together
our business on the earth would have been so happy.
More than one town would have bowed to us,
o, my own, my natural, homeless brother.

As the last streetlamp went out on the bridge,
I am a tavern tsarina, you a tavern tsar.
Swear allegiance people, to my tsar.
Swear allegiance to his tsarina – I give myself to all of you.

Yes, if only fate had brought you and I together
the royal bells would have rang out over us.
A ringing would have risen along the River Moskva,
for the fine pretender and her little friend.

Having walked long, having danced at the crazy banquet,
we would have staggered, good friend, in the night wind
and the little road would have raised such white, white dust –
if only fate had brought you and I together

The world's nomadic lands began in darkness:
trees wandering the night earth,
grapes fermenting into golden wine,
stars travelling from house to house,
rivers beginning their journey backwards,
and me hoping to sleep on your breast.

Dear companions who've spent the night with us.
Miles and miles and miles and stale bread…
The rumble of gypsy carts,
of rivers flowing backwards –
the rumble…

Ah, in the heavenly, early gypsy dawn,
do you remember the warm neighing and the steppe in silver?
Of the blue smoke on the mountain
and of the gypsy tsar –
a song…

In the black midnight, under the cover of ancient branches,
we gave you sons fine as the night,
sons wretched as the night…
and the nightingale roared loud –
with praise.

They did not hold on to you, travellers of that marvellous time,
wretched bliss and our wretched banquets.
The fires burned out brightly,
thickly down on our rugs they fell –
the stars…

UNCOLLECTED POEMS (1910-1916)

No doubt we'll meet in hell, my passionate sisters,
and we'll drink hell's pitch,
we, who with each vein
sang praises to the Lord.

We, who did not bend in the night
over the cradle or the spinning wheel,
have been carried away by an unsteady boat
under cover of a great cloak.

Dressed up since early morning
in delicate Chinese silk
we struck up heavenly songs
at the robber's camp fire.

Shoddy needlewomen
(necks mismatched and all in a mess!)
dancers and pipers,
mistresses to the whole world.

One minute scarcely covered in rags
the next our hair plaited with constellations,
both in jails and summer walkways
having strolled the heavens.

Having strolled in the starlit night
in the apple orchard in paradise
I am sure we'll meet, loved girls
dear sisters – in hell.

In order to reach lips and the bed
past God's terrifying church,
I must walk.

Past the wedding carriages,
funereal hearses.
An angelic ban has been placed
at his threshold.

Thus, in the night of moonless nights,
past the iron night-watchmen:
of sharp-sighted gates –

to the bright singing doors
through the incense of the black cloud
I will speed,

just like man hurries
from the age past God –
to man.

I shall reclaim you from all lands, from all the heavens,
because the forest is my cradle and the grave my forest,
because I stand on the earth with only one foot,
because I will sing to you like no one else.

I shall reclaim you from all times, from all nights,
all golden banners, all swords.
I shall throw away the keys and drive the dogs from the porch
because in the earthly night I am more faithful than a dog.

I shall reclaim you from all others – you, alone.
You will be nobody's bridegroom, I shall be no one's bride,
and in the final struggle you'll be silent as I seize you
from him with whom Jacob stood in the night.

But until I cross my fingers on your breast
I'm cursed to see you remain as you, wrapped up in yourself
your two wings aiming at the ether:
because the world is your cradle and your grave is the world.

PSYCHE

TO ALYA

1

I don't know where you end and I begin:
the same songs, the same worries.
That's the kind of friends we are.
That's the kind of orphans we are.

And it's so fine the two of us –
homeless, sleepless and orphaned…
Two birds: the minute we're up – we sing.
Two wanderers: we feed on the world.

2

I wander with you past
great churches and small parishes.
I wander with you past
wretched hovels and lordly manors.

Once you said: 'Buy that one!'
the Kremlin Towers having caught your eye.
The Kremlin – yours from birth. Sleep,
my first born bright and terrible.

3

And just like the grass under the earth
is friends with the iron ore,
these two bright eyes always see
the ways into the heavenly abyss.

Sibyl – Why has my child
been given such a destiny?
to endure Russia's fate…while the age
has been given to Russia…the rowan…

UNCOLLECTED POEMS (1916-1921)

TO SONECHKA

The rain knocks at my window.
The worker beats on the lathe.
I was a street singer
and you were a prince's son.

I sang about evil fate
and down from the gilded railings,
you threw neither rouble nor kopeck
but gave me a smile.

But then the old prince found out:
he stripped his son of his medal
and commanded the servant
to banish the girl from the court.

And I got drunk into that small night.
But then in the blissful world *beyond*
it was *I* who was the prince's daughter
and *you* were the street singer!

Some are created from stone, some are created from clay –
but I become silvery and glitter.
My business is treachery, my name is Marina,
I am the fleeting sea foam.

Some are created from clay, some are created from flesh –
with that comes the grave and funeral slabs...
– christened in the sea font – and in flight
with it – endlessly battered.

Through every heart, through all the nets
my wilfulness breaks through.
Do you see me – my dissolute curls?
You won't make the salt of the earth.

Breaking about your granite legs.
with every wave I rise again.
Yes, long live the foam – the happy foam –
the high sea foam.

Yesterday he still looked me in the eyes,
but now he just turns to one side.
Yesterday he sat with the birds –
but now all the larks have become ravens.

I am stupid and you are clever,
you're alive but I'm struck dumb.
O women's cry throughout the ages:
'My love, tell me what I did to you?'

And her tears are always water and blood –
in tears of blood and water she washed herself.
Love's not a mother but a stepmother –
expect no justice, no kindness there.

Boats carry the loved ones away
the white road leads them away…
and a groan is sent up the length of the earth:
'My love, tell me what I did to you?'

Yesterday he still lay at my feet,
compared me to a Chinese dynasty.
then opened out his two little hands:
life has turned out like a rusty kopeck.

And now accused of infanticide
here I stand, unloved and weak.
Still from the depths of hell I ask you:
'My love, tell me what I did to you?'

I ask the chair I ask the bed:
'Why do I suffer and struggle to live?'
'He stopped kissing – he broke you at the wheel:
 to kiss another,' they reply.

He taught me to live in the heart of the flame,
then threw me onto the icy steppe.
That's what *you*, lover did to me!
Now tell me love what *I* did to you?

There's no point arguing, you know I'm right –
I'm no longer a lover, that's quite clear.
You can be sure when love departs
death the gardener comes near.

It's just like shaking a tree –
in time the ripe apple will fall…
For everything, everything forgive me
my love – that ever, ever I did to you!

AFTER RUSSIA

There is an hour for those words.
From auditory depths
life taps out
great laws.

Perhaps from the brow
on the lover's shoulder.
Perhaps from the ray
that's invisible by day.

Our vain desire – dust that
dies as it falls upon the sheet.
A tribute to our fear
and to our dust.

So passionate, so arbitrary:
the hour – of the most silent requests.
The hour – of landless brotherhoods.
The hour – of worldwide orphanhoods.

Unfaithful love:
that cruel valley.
Hands: light and salt.
Lips: resin and blood.

I could feel the strength
of your heartbeat against my brow...
O I could crush your skull!
Come on – tell me. Who is she?

I've had it with obsessing about what you are up to!
Look here are the larks, see the honeysuckle
splashing out in handfuls everywhere.
With my wildness and calmness,
with my rainbows and tears, with my
sneaking up and muttering curses....

Life you are so dear,
still so greedy.
Don't ever forget that brow
upon the lover's shoulder.

I get up with the birds –
those twittering in the dark...
my happy greeting
in your chronicle!

EARTH OMENS

So, in the days' barren labours,
and your clumsy passion before her,
you will forget the friendly trochee
of your steadfast woman friend.

Her bitter gift of sternness,
passion concealed by shyness,
and that wireless blow
that comes in from the distance.

Everything belongs to the past, apart from *give* and *mine*.
Everything is driven by jealousy, except the mundane.
Everything belongs to faith, but in a deathly battle
with doubting Thomas.

Nezhenka! Show more respect for your past.
Don't take this woman refugee under your roof.
Long live the heart that beats like a forge
and takes you to simple places.

But perhaps, you have grown weary
of endless domestic female twittering
and you will recall my hand with no rights
and my manly arm.

Lips, not demanding receipts,
rights, not following after,
eyes, unable to control eyelids
exploring the light.

Nighttime whispers: a hand
and the rustle of silk.
Nighttime whispers: lips
and the smoothness of silk.
Paid back for petty jealousies
fired up with old scores
jaws tightened –
and then
an argument –
it died down
in the rustling…
and there's a leaf
in the pane…
and the whistles of the first bird.
How pure – then a sigh.
It's not the one. The moment's gone.
I went.
A shrug
of the shoulders.
Nothing.
Vanity.
The end.
As if it didn't happen.

And in this vanity of vanities
comes a sword: the dawn.

Find yourself friends who are trusting,
the kind who still believe in miracles.
I know that Venus – is a business of hands.
I am an artisan and I know my trade.

From the highest creative muteness
to the full trampling of the soul,
all along God's stairway – from:
my breath – to: don't breathe!

Remember the law:
here we don't rule.
Then we can be
in this City of Friends:

this empty,
severe male sky
is completely covered
in gold.

In this world where rivers run backwards,
on the river bank
one imaginary hand
takes another ...

The light crackle of a spark:
an explosion and one in reply.
(False hands concealed
beneath handshakes).

O this friendly fluttering
of clothes smooth as sword –
in the sky of male gods,
in the sky of male celebrations.

Thus, between adolescences:
between equalities,
dawn in fresh latitudes,
in the sunburn of the games –

greetings on the dry wind,
souls free of passion.
In the sky of Tarpeian slopes
in the sky of Spartan friendships.

A time will come Lord
when my life acquires
the tranquillity of grey hair,
the tranquillity of the heights

and in the first silence
of that first blueness,
I will reach the high shoulder
that has endured everything in life.

And it will be only you Lord,
only you, not any of you others,
like when I tore away from the
downy clouds into the mountain blue.

As like sleep beneath stubborn lips
I listened to the grass…
(Here, on the earth of arts,
I am reputed to be a bard.)

And how weary I am
of lies – those packhorse dues,
like from the last veins
comes the first quiver in the forest…

OPHELIA TO HAMLET

Hamlet, doubled up in thought,
a sickly shadow beneath his halo
of knowledge and doubts...
(When *was* that play published?)

I'm immune to your abuse and emptiness,
spawned from your festering, adolescent den.
You have already lain on this breast
like some weighty chronicle.

Chaste woman hater! (Why did they indulge
this absurd chosen one?) Did you once
think about what was plucked
from the small flower garden of madness...

Roses? But — shh — that is surely the future.
We pick them and new ones grow. Did the roses
ever betray us? Did they betray lovers
and were there then less of them?

Having been fulfilled, having been fragrant you will drown,
never existed... But you will remember us,
at that moment when over the flowing river chronicle
Hamlet with all your intensity you come once more into being.

OPHELIA IN DEFENCE OF THE QUEEN

Prince Hamlet, stop disturbing
the worm-eaten bed. Look at the roses.
Think of her and that this is the last
of her remaining days.

Prince Hamlet, stop discrediting the womb
of the queen. It is not for the chaste to stand judge
over passion. Phaedra is much guiltier,
and they have been singing about her to this very day.

And they always will. But you, with your dash of chalk
and decay…your malignant gossip with bones,
Prince Hamlet, it's not your job to judge those
who are driven by passion. But if you do…

I defy you to…run across the flagstones
up into the bedchamber to do your worst:
I, your immortal passion,
rise in defence of my queen.

PHAEDRA

1

THE COMPLAINT

Hippolytus, Hippolytus, It hurts.
It's so hot, my cheeks are burning...
What sort of cruel terror is hidden
in this name Hippolytus?.

Like the wave that batters the granite rocks
without end, I am engulfed
by the flames of Hippolytus,
driven mad and enslaved by Hippolytus.

Arms want to be ripped from their sockets
and flung into the earth, teeth want to grind stones
into dust — O, to weep and lie down together:
I'm consumed by this passion in my head...

Herculaneum dust is trapped in my lips
and my nostrils...I'm fading... going
blind...it's drier than sand and ashes:
Hippolytus – it's worse than saws!

It's a horsefly in the visible weeping
of a splashing wound...a horsefly getting
agitated – a young mare in flames,
a galloping red wound.

Hippolytus. Hippolytus. Hide me
in this *peplos* as into a crypt:
Elysium for old nags, ready
to be flayed – the horsefly burns.

Hippolytus, Hippolytus. I want to be
your prisoner – not this Harpy's beak
in my breasts, in my hot spring. How I long
for the petalled caress of Hippolytus.

Hippolytus, Hippolytus. I need to drink!
Son or stepson, you are still my accomplice.
This is lava not slabs beneath my feet –
Could it be Olympus stirring?

Such sleepy-faced Olympians.
We sculpt the gods.
Hippolytus. Hippolytus. Wrap me in a cloak.
In this *peplos*, as into a crypt.

Hippolytus, ease my pain…

2

THE MESSAGE

To Hippolytus from his mother, Queen Phaedra, comes news.
To the inconstant boy, whose beauty runs from Phaedra
like wax from powerful Phoebus…moans from
her impassioned lips: to Hippolytus from Phaedra.

Soothe my soul. It's impossible to soothe the soul
without touching lips. Impossible to touch lips
without touching Psyche, that fluttering guest of lips…
Soothe my soul, and thus soothe my lips.

Hippolytus, I am tired. This is not simple brazenness, but
the shame of whores and priestesses crying out to you.
Speeches and hands may be simple but behind such quivering
lies a great secret on which silence places a finger.

Forgive me virgin, adolescent, horseman, hater of bliss.
It isn't lust. It isn't the whim of a woman's heart.
It may be a seducer. It may be Psyche cajoling us
to listen close to the babblings of Hippolytus.

'You should be ashamed,' they say, but it's too late – one final
splash and my horses have bolted – over the sheer drop to dust…
Yet I am a horsewoman too as I fall from the precipice,
the two fatal hills of my breasts, into your chest's abyss –

(Is it not mine?) – Do it more bravely, more tenderly
than into a small wax board. Isn't the heart's wax dark?
Using a stylus to cut out the symbols
let Hippolytus's secret be read by the lips of

your insatiable Phaedra.

EURYDICE TO ORPHEUS

For those cut off from the last fragments
of the shroud (no more lips or cheeks…)
is there not some excess of power
in Orpheus descending into Hades?

For those who have given up the last earthly
ties here at last on the bed of all beds,
we no longer need to detect the lies in
the outer world, we can look within to –

a knife meeting – cut to a generous fit,
the freedom of immortality has been paid for
with roses of blood…
                You who have loved
to the very heart of Lethe must allow me the peace

of forgetfulness – for in this ghostly house
you who are alive are the ghost, while I, though dead,
am more real…What else can I say to you except:
'You must forget this and leave.'

You can no longer make me feel – I won't be drawn in,
after all I have no hands, no lips to kiss with –
women's passion ends with the immortality
of the serpent's sting.

This endless expanse has been paid for –
and don't you ever forget it.
Orpheus you don't need to come down to Eurydice –
no need for brothers to disturb sisters.

POETS

1

The poet — brings speech from far off.
Speech — carries the poet far.

By planets, by omens, along the muddy tracks
of hidden parables...Between *yes* and *no*
he avoids a detour with a spectacular leap
from the bell tower...For the path of comets —

is the path of poets, breaking the chains
of causality — this is what ties him. Don't even try to
look up, you will only despair, for poets' eclipses
are not predictable by the calendar.

He is the one who shuffles the cards,
who cheats with weights and measures,
who seeks answers from books,
who out-argues Kant.

The one who lies in the stone grave of the Bastille
like a tree in its beauty,
the one whose tracks always disappear without trace,
the train for whom everyone
is late...
                   for the path of comets

is the path of poets: burning without warming,
he reaps before he sows, explosion and forced entry —
your pathway is long maned and crooked,
not predicted by the calendar.

2

In the world you'll find the superfluous…
the surplus to requirements, the unnoticed,
(whose names remain unrecorded,
for them a rubbish heap is home).

In the world you'll find the hollow ones,
the downtrodden, the dumb – just dirt,
or a nail that catches on your silk skirt,
mud defiled beneath your wheels.

In the world you'll find the invisible ones,
the insubstantial: (you'll recognise them
by their leprosy spots). There are
in the world Jobs who would envy Job –

and likewise there is us…the poets, rhyming pariahs…
yet having been thrown up on the flood
we try to win god from the goddesses
and a virgin from the gods.

3

What shall I do, blind and a stepson,
in a world, where everyone can see and has a father,
where passions travel along curses like
along an embankment, where tears
are called a cold?

What shall I do, built and trained to be
a singer – like a wire, sunburn or Siberia!
Travelling my delusions as if along a bridge,
with their weightlessness
in a world of weight?

What shall I do, singer and first born
in a world where the most black is grey,
where inspiration is kept as in a thermos
with this measurelessness
in a world of measures?

A DIALOGUE BETWEEN HAMLET AND HIS CONSCIENCE

She is on the bottom, where there is silt
and water plants…she went to sleep in them –
but it is not possible to sleep there.
But I loved her
like forty thousand brothers
could not love her.
                    Hamlet.

She is on the bottom, where there is
silt…silt! And the last garland
has appeared on the riverside logs.
But I loved her like forty thousand…
                              less,
all the same, than a single lover.

But she is on the bottom, where there is silt.
But did I –
        (*perplexed*)
                love her?

MAGDALENE

1

Between us the Ten Commandments,
the heat of ten campfires.
My own blood recoils –
you are alien blood to me.

In gospel times
I would have been one of those...
(alien blood – is the most wished for
and most alien of all)

who would have been drawn to you,
who would have reached out to you
in my weakness, in my gaudy colours,
languishing with demonic eyes.

I would pour oils over and under your feet,
letting them flow onto the sands...
Passion sold off, spat out
by merchants – see it flow.

With the moisture from my lips,
the scales of my eyes and
in the sweat of all voluptuousness...
I wrap your feet in my hair, as in fur.

I spread myself like some cloth
beneath your feet...for I am she,
while you are the one who said to
her with the flaming curls: arise sister.

2

Ointments bought for three times
their value, the sweat of passion,
tears, hair – an endless
pouring forth, while he

stood, his blessed gaze fixed
down into the dry red clay:
Magdalene, Magdalene!
Don't be so free with yourself.

3

I shall not torment you for what you do.
Dear one, everything has come to pass.
I was barefoot, but you put shoes on my feet
with downpours of hair
and tears.

I do not ask you how much
these purchases of oil cost.
I was naked, and with sweeps of
your body, you enclosed me
like a wall.

I will touch your nakedness with my fingers
more silent than water and lower than grass.
I was upright and you caused me to bend
after clinging so close with tenderness.

Dig me a pit in your hair.
Swaddle me without flax.
Bearer of ointments what's linen to me?
You washed me
like a wave.

AN ATTEMPT AT JEALOUSY

So what's it like
living with some other woman?
Simpler is it? With just one stroke of the oar
can the memory of me, an island
floating in the sky not on the water,

have so quickly faded like
a receding shoreline…?
O souls, souls,
we should be sisters –
never lovers.

What's it like living
with an ordinary woman,
one who lacks the divine,
since (like you) your queen
has come down from her throne?

What's it like?
How do you eat, get up,
get about? Being so
ordinary and banal
how do you cope, poor man?

'I've had it up to here with all this!
I must get my own place' – .
What's it like living with
any old person
you my chosen one?

Is the food more edible?
Does it suit you better?
(You can't complain if it makes you sick).
What's it like living with a mere semblance –
you who have walked on Sinai?

What's it like living with
a stranger to these parts?
Tell me straight, do you love her?
Or does Zeus's shame
hang upon your brow?

What's it like?
Can you possibly be in good health?
How do you sing?
With all that festering guilt on your conscience
how do you cope poor man?

What's it like living
with trash from the market?
Are you paying the price?
After Carrara marble
What's it like living with crumbling plaster?

(God was carved out of a block
and has been completely destroyed.)
What's it like living with some
run-of-the mill woman,
you who have known Lilith?

Have you had enough of the latest
from the market? Has the novelty worn off?
What's it like living with
some earthly woman
without six senses?

Now, in all honesty are you happy?
No. No? What's it like living in
your bottomless pit my love?
Is it worse or the same
as my life with someone else?

UNCOLLECTED POEMS (1921-1941)

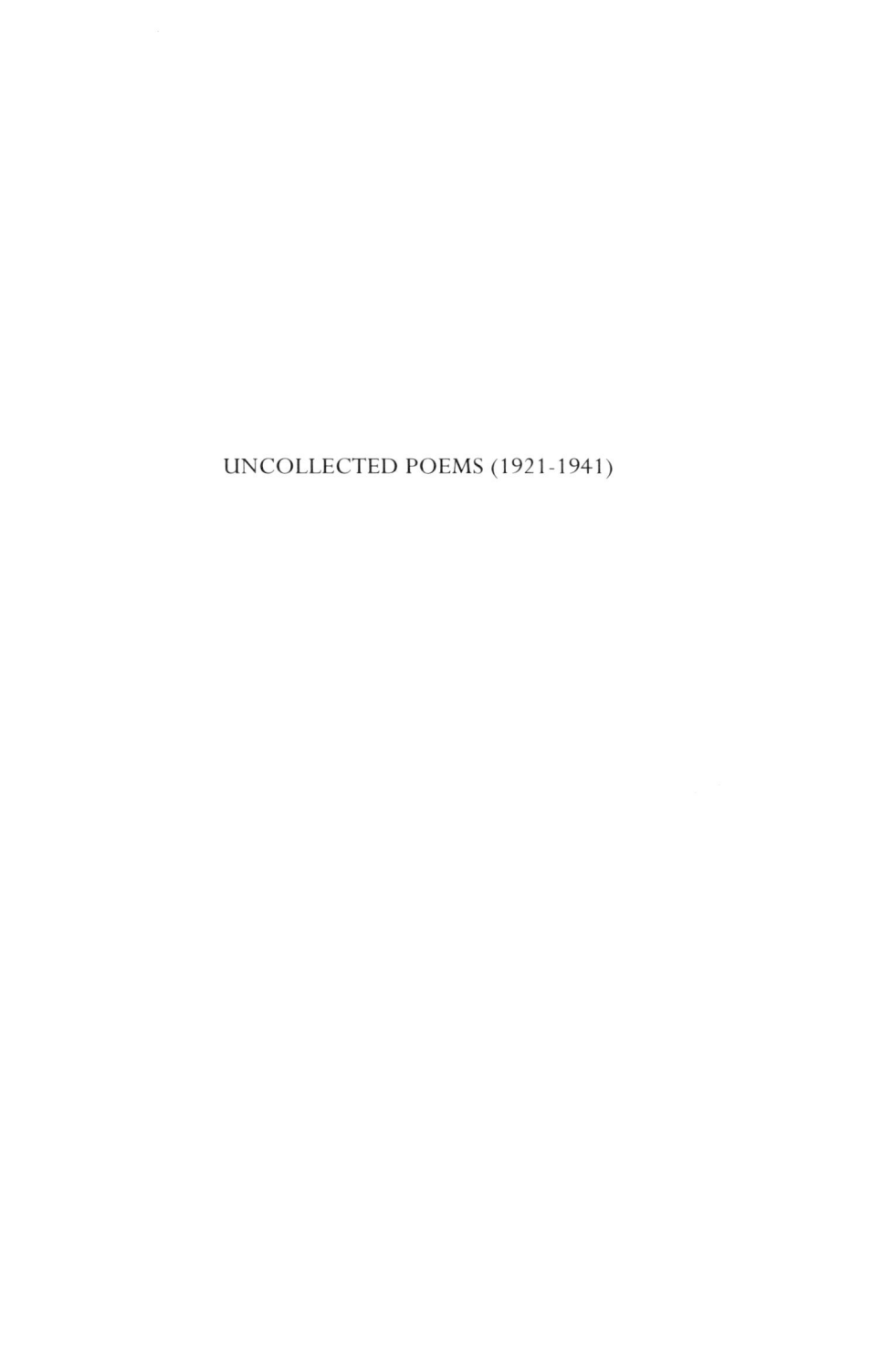

LONGING FOR HOME

The longing for home,
that all too familiar ache....
It's all the same to me where
I am to be so completely

alone, as I make my way home over
the stones from the market with my basket
to a house that is no more my own
than a hospital or barracks.

It's all the same to me among whose
faces I am to bristle like a captive
lion, and what power will be used to
distance me from myself, from my essence

like a Kamchatka bear driven off the ice
and where I won't waste my time trying to
get on with people and where I will
abase myself – it's all the same to me.

I am not deceived by my native language,
its milky call. It makes no difference to me
on what misunderstanding I am
with those I meet:

(newspaper readers, devourers of
trivial gossip) they come from
the twentieth century but me –
I reach every age.

Rooted on the spot like a log
left in some alley,
everyone's the same, it's all the same
and, perhaps even more

my own past most of all.
Everything about me, all markers,
all dates — are as if wiped clean:
the soul that was born *somewhere*.

For my country did not protect me
so that even the sharpest detective
would find no birth-mark
wherever he looked.

Each house is alien to me, each church is empty
and it's all the same and all is one...
But then...perhaps, along the road I'll see
a bush rise up, especially the rowan....

POEMS TO CZECHOSLOVAKIA

4

TO GERMANY

O, red-cheeked maiden
among the green mountains –
Germany.
Germany.
Germany.
It's a disgrace.

Astral soul, you have
pocketed half the world.
In olden times – you were dimmed with fairytales,
but now – you have gone with your tanks.

Why don't you lower your eyes
before the Czech peasant woman
as you roll in with your tanks
along the rye of her hopes?

What do you feel, Germans
before the misfortunes
of that *tiny* country:
you sons of Germany?

O mania. O mummified
grandeur.
Germany.
You will be consumed in flames.
You will create nothing but
madness,
madness.

The strongman will deal with
the boa constrictor's embrace.
Your health, Moravia.
Slovakia, remain Slovakian.
Get ready to fight
as you leave for the crystal mines:
Bohemia.
Bohemia.
Bohemia.
Nazdar !

THEY TOOK...

Czechs went up to Germans and spat
newspaper quote March 1939)

They took quickly and they took generously:
they took the mountains and they took the depths,
they took our coal and they took our steel,
and our lead, and our crystal.

They took the sugar, and they took the clover,
they took the West and they took the North,
they took the honey and they took the wheat,
they took our South and our East.

They took our spas and the Tatra Mountains,
they took nearby and faraway,
but more hurtful than taking our earthly heaven,
they took the battle – into our very homeland.

They took the bullets and took the guns,
they took the iron-ore and they took our friendships...
but while there's still saliva in our mouths,
the whole country is armed!

8

What tears in our eyes now.
This grief of anger and love.
Czechoslovakia in tears.
Spain in blood.

O Black Mountain –
you've eclipsed all the light.
It's time, its time, to return –
the ticket to the creator.

I refuse to live
in this inhuman bedlam.
I refuse to howl
with the wolves of the square.

I refuse to swim
with the sharks of the plains,
below with their backs to the current –
I refuse to be.

I need neither hearing
nor prophetic eyes.
To your mad world, there's only
one reply – refusal.

It's time to remove the amber,
it's time to change the words,
it's time to put out the lamp
over the door…

        February 1941

NOTES AND BIBLIOGRAPHY

NOTES

CONTENTS
Poems asterisked indicate poems which don't belong to a collection as published but which I have included because they belong to particular sequences.

EVENING ALBUM
In Paris: Tsvetaeva was obsessed with Napoleon at the time of this poem. Edmond Rostand (1868-1918) was the French playwright who wrote *Cyrano de Bergerac* and *L'Aiglon* which is about Napoleon's only son the Duke of Reichstadt. Sarah refers to Sarah Bernhardt whom Tsvetaeva admired as a result of seeing her in Ronstand's play. Tsvetaeva went on to translate the whole play but it has not been preserved.

POEMS OF YOUTH
To Sergey Efron-Durnovo: dedicated to her husband Sergey Efron who she married in 1912.

A Woman Friend: This sequence is dedicated to the poet Sophia Parnok (1885-1933) with whom she had a very open affair in 1914. *Today at seven, the sleighs headed off*: 'Oh, je n'en puis plus, j'etouffe!' 'I can't take any more, I'm choking!'; Kay is a character from Hans Christian Anderson's *The Snow Queen*.

VERSTS
This title of this volume refers to the Russian measurement of approx 1.06 km. It is also the word for road markers to indicate this distance, hence the collection being translated as *Milestones* by some translators.

No one has taken anything away and *You throw back your head*: These two poems are dedicated to Osip Mandelstam (1891-1938) one of Russia's greatest twentieth century poets; Derzhavin a great Russian poet (1743-1816).

Four years old: golubka is a term of endearment meaning literally my little pigeon, taken to mean my dear.

Poems about Moscow: Clouds – all around: *Vagankova* is a cemetery in Moscow. *Take from my hands, my strange and beautiful brother*; The *Spassky Gates* and the chapel housing the icon *Unexpected Joy* are both in the Kremlin; *Squares hurry us past*: The *Iverskaya Chapel* containing another sacred icon stands at the entrance to Red Square; *The bells rain down on the blue groves*: Kaluga Province is south of Moscow and Tsvetaeva regularly stayed in this province in semi-rural Tarusa as a child; *The rowan tree blazed up:* The feast day of St John the Divine, the day Tsvetaeva, was born is 26th September.

Insomnia: Insomnia is a common theme in Russian poetry. See Michael Wachtel's *The Cambridge Introduction to Russian Poetry* for a discussion of this subject. *Insomnia my friend*: *lastochka moia* is a term of endearment meaning literally my little swallow.

Poems to Alexander Blok: Tsvetaeva idolised Alexander Blok who was the leading poet of the Symbolists. He died before she had a chance to get to know him (1880-1921) though she did go to one of his readings.

Poems to Akhmatova: *I stand here with my head in my hands*: Anna Akhmatova (1889-1966) ranks with Osip Mandelstam as one of Russia's greatest twentieth century poets; Tsarskoe Selo is a the location of the tsars' palace just outside St Petersburg associated with Pushkin and somewhere familiar to Akhmatova from childhood; *The name of the child is Lev*: Lev is the name of Akhmatova's son and also the Russian for lion or its diminiutive *levenka*.

UNCOLLECTED POEMS (1910-1916)
I shall reclaim you from all lands, from all the heavens: *You'll be silent as I seize you/from him with whom Jacob stood in the night.* This 'him' refers to God. It is a reference to the biblical story where Jacob wrestled with God in the night and only agreed to end the fight if God blessed him. As a result God named him Israel and he became the father of the Jewish nation.

PSYCHE
To Alya: This poem is dedicated to Tsvetaeva's daughter; The Sibyl refers to a prophetess of classical mythology. Elsewhere Tsvetaeva has a sequence dedicated to her.

UNCOLLECTED POEMS (1916-1921)
To Sonechka: This poem is dedicated to Sofia Gollidey (1894-1934) an actress Tsvetaeva met in 1919. They had an intense friendship for a short period and Tsvetaeva dedicated many plays and poems to her. Unlike the very destructive relationship she had with Parnok this remained platonic and was also always recalled fondly by Tsvetaeva.

Yesterday he still looked me in the eyes: In the line 'I stand accused of infanticide' Tsvetaeva is making reference to the death of her daughter Irina that took place 2/3 February 1920. This poem was written 14 June 1920 when this event would still have been very raw. It provides clear evidence of Tsvetaeva being prepared to engage with the dark side in her verse. The backdrop to this statement is the various rumours that abounded with regards Tsvetaeva's alleged neglect of this child who did not show the same precociousness as the older daughter Alya.

AFTER RUSSIA
Earth Omens: nezhenka a term used to describe someone who is mollycoddled.

Remember the law: Tarpeian Rock. Famous rock in Rome from which traitors were thrown.

Phaedra: Phaedra fell in love with her stepson Hippolytus. On her rejection by him, she brought about his death by slandering him to her husband Theseus. She subsequently killed herself in remorse. *The Complaint*: a *peplos* is a robe consisting of a large rectangular piece of cloth that would have been woven and given as an annual gift to Athena and then worn as a robe on a life size statue.

Eurydice to Orpheus: Eurydice is married to Orpheus but is killed by a serpent when fleeing from the attentions of Aristaeus. Orpheus while looking for her in Hades charmed Pluto with his music who then promised to return her to him if he did not look back until they had returned to the upper world. Inevitably he looks back and Eurydice is forced to remain in Hades.

Poets: In the world you'll find the superfluous...: Job represents poverty and patience. God inflicts terrible punishment on him to test his piety. In spite of illness and losing his wealth, family and friends he refuses to curse God. Ultimately God rewards him by returning everything to him.

An Attempt at Jealousy: This poem is believed to be dedicated to Konstantin Rodzevich (1895-1988) with whom, in 1923, Tsvetaeva had one of her most intense affairs. It lasted about three months and she suffered a great deal at the break up. For Efron this was the closest they came to separating; *Mount Sinae*: the mountain where God gave Moses The Ten Commandments; *Carrara Marble*: Carrara is a town in Italy where this white marble is made. *Lilith*: the first wife of Adam according to rabbinical writings. She is also variously presented as a monster or vampire-like figure who haunts wildernesses and is particularly dangerous to children.

UNCOLLECTED POEMS (1921-1941)
Longing for Home: Kamchatka is a very remote area in Russia.

To Germany: Like many other exiles Tsvetaeva lived a number of years in Czechoslovakia and was also one of the many Russians who received stipends from the Czech government after the Russian Civil War; *nazdar* is a Czech word meaning both hallo and goodbye.

It's time to remove the amber: During Tsvetaeva's last few months before her suicide in the face of overall depression, apparently, her one comfort was a piece of amber jewellery which she wore.

BIBLIOGRAPHY

Braithwaite, Rodric. *Moscow 1941: A City and its People at War*. London: Profile 2006.

Carlisle, Olga. *Poets on Street Corners: Portraits of Fifteen Russian poets*. New York: Random House. 1970.

Ciepiela, Catherine. *The Same Solitude: Boris Pasternak and Marina Tsvetaeva*. Ithaca: Cornell Univ. Press. 2006.

Clark, Alan. *Barbarossa: the Russian-German Conflict 1941-1945*. London: Cassall Military Paperbacks. repr. 2005.

Dinega, Alyssa, W. *A Russian Psyche: the Poetic Mind of Marina Tsvetaeva*. Madison: Univ. of Wisconsin Press. 2001.

Efron, Georgy. *Dnevnizi v Dvukh Tomax: 1940-1943 Godi. (Diaries in Two Volumes: 1940-41)*: Moscow: Vagrius. 2005.

Feinstein, Elaine. *A Captive Lion. The Life of Marina Tsvetaeva*. London, 1987.

Hasty, Olga, p. *Tsvetaeva's Orphic Journeys in the Worlds of the Word*. Evanston: Northwestern Univ. press. 1996.

Karlinsky, Simon. *Marina Cvetaeva. Her Life and Art*. Berkeley and Los Angeles, 1966.

——————. *Marina Tsvetaeva. The Woman, her World and her Poetry*. Cambridge univ. Press, 1985.

Kudrova, Irma. *The Death of a Poet: the Last Days of Marina Tsvetaeva*. trans. Mary Ann Szporluk. London: Overlook Duckworth. 2004.

Pasternak, Yegeny and Yelena Pasternak and Konstantin Azadovsky eds. *Letters, Summer 1926: Boris Pasternak, Marina Tsvetaeva, Rainer Maria Rilke*. trans. Margaret Wettlin and Walter Arndt. New York: Harcourt Brace Jovanovich. 1985.

Proffer, Ellendea. ed. *Tsvetaeva: A Pictorial Biography*. trans. J. Martin King. Ann Arbor: Ardis, 1980.

Razumovsky, Maria. *Marina Tsvetaeva: A Critical Introduction*. trans. Aleksey Gibson Newcastle upon Tyne: Bloodaxe books. 1994.

Schweitzer, Victoria. *Tsvetaeva*. trans. Robert Chandler, H.T. Willets and (poetry) Peter Norman. ed. Angela Livingstone. London: Harvill. 1988.

Taubman, Jane. *A Life through Poetry. Marina Tsvetaeva's Lyric Diary*. Columbus: Slavica Publishers. 1989.

Tsvetaeva, Marina. *Stikhotvorenia i poemy v pyati tomakh*. (Lyric and narrative poems in five volumes). ed. Alexander Sumerkin. New York: Russica Publishers. 1980.

——————. *Sobranie Sochinenia v semi tomax*. (Collected Works in Seven volumes). ed. Anna Saakyants and L'va Mnukhina. Moscow: Ellis Lak. 1994.

——————. *Selected Poems*. trans. Elaine Feinstein. Oxford: Univ. Press. 1971.

——————. *Selected Poems*. trans. David Mcduff. Newcastle upon Tyne: Bloodaxe Books. 1987.

——————. *Milestones*. trans. Robin Kemball. Evanston: Northwestern Univ. Press. 2003.

——————. *Poem of the End: Selected Narrative and Lyrical Poems*. trans. Nina Kossman, with Andrew Newcomb. New York: Ardis Publishers. 2004.

——————. *After Russia*. trans. Michael Naydan with Slava Yastremski. Ann Arbor: Ardis Publishers. 1992.

——————. *A Captive Spirit: Selected Prose*. ed. J. Marin King. London: Virago Press. 1983.

——————. *Art in the Light of Conscience: Eight Essays on Poetry by Marina Tsvetaeva*. trans. Angela Livingstone. Cambridge: Harvard University Press. 1992

Wachtel, Michael. *The Cambridge Introduction to Russian Poetry*. Cambridge University Press. 2004.

White, Mary Jane. *Starry Sky to Starry Sky: Poems by Mary Jane White with Translations by Marina Tsveteaeva*. Stevens Point: Holy Cow! Press. 1988.

Worple Press is an independent publishing house that specialises in poetry, art and alternative titles.

Worple Press can be contacted at:
PO Box 328, Tonbridge, Kent TN9 1WR Tel 01732 368 958
email: theworpleco@aol.com.
website: www.worplepress.co.uk

Trade orders: Central Books, 99 Wallis Road, London E9 5LN
Tel 0845 5489911

TITLES INCLUDE:

Against Gravity – **Beverley Brie Brahic**
(A5 Price £8.00 ISBN 1-905208-03-0, pp. 72)

Full Stretch – **Anthony Wilson**
(Price £10 / 15 Euros ISBN 1-905208-04-9, pp. 104)

Bearings – **Joseph Woods**
(A5 Price £8.00 / 10 Euros ISBN 1-905208-00-6, pp. 64)

'his work shows an impressive reach and range'   *Eiléan Ní Chuilleanáin*

'good and interesting poems well-presented'   *Books Ireland*

A Ruskin Alphabet – **Kevin Jackson**
(A6 Price £4.50 ISBN 0-9530947-2-3, pp. 88)

'you may like to consult *A Ruskin Alphabet* by Kevin Jackson, a collection of facts and opinions on ruskin and Ruskinites, together with a variety of pithy remarks from the man himself'   *TLS*

Looking In All Directions – **Peter Kane Dufault**
(A5 Price £10.00 ISBN 0-9530947-5-8, pp. 188)

'Wonderful stuff'   *Ted Hughes*

The Great Friend and Other Translated Poems – **Peter Robinson**
(A5 Price £8.00 ISBN 0-9530947-7-4, pp. 75)

Poetry Book Society Recommended Translation

The Verbals – **Kevin Jackson in Conversation with Iain Sinclair**
(A5 Price £12.00 / 20 Euros ISBN 0-9530947-9-0, pp. 148)

'Highly interesting.'   *The Guardian*

'Cultists will be eager to get their hands on it.'   *TLS*

Stigmata – **Clive Wilmer**
(A5 Price £10.00 / 15 Euros ISBN 1-905208-01-4, pp. 28)

'a brilliant piece of work which brings honour to our time'
Sebastian Barker

Bowl – **Elizabeth Cook**
(A5 Price £10.00 / 15 Euros ISBN 1-905208-09-X, pp. 84)

'eloquent and profoundly humane'   *Martha Kapos*

A Suite for Summer – **John Freeman**
(A5 Price £10.00 / 15 Euros ISBN 978-1-905208-10-4, pp. 78)

'His poetry re-awakens a sense of wonder in us'   *Kim Taplin*

To Be in The Same World – **Peter Kane Dufault**
(A5 Price £10.00 / 15 Euros $20 ISBN 978-1-905208-07-4, pp. 94)

'as fresh and valuable as ever'   *George Szirtes (Poetry Review)*

FORTHCOMING TITLES

Warp and Weft — **an anthology of Worple writing**

Foraging: New and Selected Poems — **James Aitchison**

Home GAME

LISA SUZANNE

HOME GAME
VEGAS ACES BOOK ONE
© 2021 Lisa Suzanne

All rights reserved. In accordance with the US Copyright Act of 1976, the scanning, uploading, and sharing of any part of this book without the permission of the publisher or author constitute unlawful piracy and theft of the author's intellectual property. No part of this book may be reproduced or transmitted in any form or by any means, electronic or mechanical, including photocopying, recording, or by any information storage and retrieval system without the written permission of the author, except where permitted by law and except for excerpts used in reviews. If you would like to use any words from this book other than for review purposes, prior written permission must be obtained from the publisher.

Published in the United States of America by Books by LS, LLC.

ISBN: 9798707092992

This book is a work of fiction. Any similarities to real people, living or dead, is purely coincidental. All characters and events in this work are figments of the author's imagination.

Cover Designed by Najla Qamber Designs
Content Editing by It's Your Story Content Editing
Proofreading by Proofreading by Katie

Home GAME

BOOKS BY LISA SUZANNE

A LITTLE LIKE DESTINY SERIES
A Little Like Destiny (Book One)
Only Ever You (Book Two)
Clean Break (Book Three)

MY FAVORITE BAND STANDALONES
Take My Heart
The Benefits of Bad Decisions
Waking Up Married
Driving Me Crazy
It's Only Temporary
The Replacement War

Visit Lisa on Amazon for more titles

DEDICATION

To the three who make my *Home Game* the most fun.

CHAPTER 1

"Come on, Todd," I murmur. "It's fine. Nobody will ever know."

"Not at work," he mutters. He shuffles some papers on his desk just after his eyes flick to my chest. He wants this too, clearly, and his words of protest are more along the obligatory line than the sincere one.

I'm not usually the girl who comes onto her colleague at work, but we've been dating for the last few months, and last night he railed me good and hard, so this girl is back for her seconds.

I walk around his desk, and he looks up at me. I look down at him. That moment of *yeah this is happening* passes between us, and I take that as my signal.

I hike up my skirt and climb onto his lap.

His hands settle onto my ass, and he shifts me around a little, letting me know he's into it too. Gone are the weak protests of a moment ago, instead replaced by the tiny kisses he's trailing up my neck.

I lean back to give him more space to work with, and I shiver a little at how good it feels. He shifts his hips up toward me, and I buck mine down, and that's the good ol' signal that we're about to bang.

"I don't have a condom," he whispers. His eyes dart toward the door.

"I do," I say, but it's in my purse tucked into my desk drawer in my office. I nip a kiss on his lips. "Be right back."

I climb off him and scurry to my office, grab the condom out of my purse, and rush back.

Belinda, our boss, is standing in the doorway when I return. Her eyes fall to me, and I tighten my fist around the condom in my palm. I wish I wasn't wearing a dress with no pockets today. Why do I even own a dress without pockets? How terribly inconvenient.

"How's the Montgomery account coming?" she asks, raising a brow at me.

"Excellent," I lie. Truth be told, I've barely even glanced at the Montgomery account. She just slid it into my inbox this morning. I had some other things I was wrapping up and then I wanted to wrap up Todd and *then* I was going to dig into it.

She purses her lips like she doesn't believe me, and I smile. She doesn't like me. The feeling is mutual.

"What are you doing in Todd's office?" she prods.

"I just wanted to run a few things by him regarding the construction company you gave us," I say. It's not a total lie. That's what brought me here in the first place, but sex—or at least the promise of it—is what kept me here a little longer.

"Fine. Then back to your office, and I want a summary of your plans for Montgomery before you leave today."

I smile sweetly even though I'm now seething on the inside. Before I leave today? That'll make for a long night, but most nights at this job are long. At least I like what I do...even if I don't like my boss. "Of course."

She stomps off, and I look at Todd and make a face. I kick the door shut behind me and stalk toward the guy who's about to make my eyes roll to the back of my head.

"Now where were we?" I ask, settling back onto his lap and linking my arms around his neck.

He chuckles. "I was just getting back to work. I've got deadlines and as much fun as this sounds, I don't think we should do it at work. Let's save it for later when we can take our time."

I thrust my hips down on him again. "You sure about that?"

He groans, and then he mutters, "Nope. Not even a little." And then he gives me what I want. I produce the condom from my palm and shift back. He glances at the door, and then he sighs, unzips his pants, pulls himself out, and rolls on the condom.

I feel giddy as he reaches toward me and hooks his finger around my panties to shove them aside before he thrusts up into me.

I moan—loudly—and he presses his mouth to mine in some misguided attempt to quiet me, and then he really starts moving.

It's hot and illicit doing this here in his office. It's bright outside so no one can see in, especially not up here on the fifth floor, but I can see out there, and I see cars moving and people walking while I'm up here getting screwed in a desk chair.

I throw my head back and close my eyes, giving into the heat and passion that burns between us.

"Oh God," I moan. "Oh yes, yes, yes!" He clamps a hand over my mouth, but it's too late. I'm yelling because holy hell he's good at the sex stuff, and he keeps hammering into me because neither of us are done yet, except I'm just about done because he feels so damn good. I start yelling as everything goes black and pleasure is just about to sweep over me. "I'm so close, so close!"

And then he gasps and everything stops as I'm about to fly into my orgasm. I'm dying for just a teeny-tiny little more friction to really send this bliss to that sheer level of perfection, and he's thick inside me but completely still.

I open my eyes to see just why the hell he thought it was a good idea to stop moving as my body is literally tipping over the edge of ecstasy, and I see his wide eyes pinned toward the door.

My heart stops for a beat as my brain catches up, and then my head slowly turns to see what caused him to stop.

He shifts as I turn, and it's just enough of a shift to tip me into the throes of my climax as my eyes meet Belinda's across the room.

I cry out as I fly headfirst into my orgasm. I close my eyes tight and come and come as I grip onto Todd, and then it all stops, and I'm pretty sure Belinda saw the entire thing.

And now what?

Do I just, you know, climb off him? Because then that big, hard thing will just be hanging out for Belinda to see.

"I'll give you a minute," she says, and then the door slams shut.

"Do, uh..." I pause. "Do you want to finish?"

"Um, no." He gently pushes me off, but I was really just thinking of him. You know, blue balls and all that. "Dammit, Ellie. I told you we shouldn't do it at work."

"Oh, so now this is *my* fault?" I fire back as I smooth my dress back into place and attempt to balance myself as my knees still shake from that orgasm.

He pulls off the condom and tucks himself back into his pants. He grabs a tissue to get rid of it. "I didn't say that, exactly, but yes. It's absolutely your fault. You didn't even bother to lock the door?"

I lift a shoulder. "Guess not. But you could've put up a fight if you really didn't want to do it."

"Are you serious right now? If I did put up a fight, you would've badgered me until you got your way anyway. I love this job, and you didn't lock the door, and now we'll probably both be fired for having sex in the workplace during working hours, and man you didn't just fuck me, but you somehow managed to fuck me over, too." He heaves out a breath when he finishes his speech.

I stare at him with wide eyes, not really sure what to say to that. "Really, Todd?" My comeback is weak, but the truth of the matter remains: Todd is no Prince Charming, and it looks like our relationship was no fairy tale.

There's a knock on the door.

"Come in," Todd yells.

Belinda shakes her head in disgust when she opens the door.

I've been working here for three years, starting as an intern fresh out of college and working my way up to account manager. Belinda was brought over from a competing company a few months ago and we sort of got off on the wrong foot.

"Well, he's right," she says, not hiding the fact that she heard our entire conversation through the door. "You're both fired."

I guess it looks like Belinda and I will be *ending* things on the wrong foot, too.

CHAPTER 2

"And that's the story of how I lost my boyfriend and my job in the same day," I finish.

My brother laughs. "Only you, Ellie, I swear."

I hold the phone between my ear and my shoulder as I grab my suitcase down from my closet shelf.

"Are you still coming Thursday?" he asks.

"Yep," I say. "I need a weekend away now more than ever, to be honest. I'm not really all that sad about Todd. He was hot, and I had hope for us at the start, but it turns out he was just a crush. It's not like I saw myself marrying him or anything. And the job...well, I've never been fired before, so that kind of stings. But I'll find something."

"Move to Vegas," he says softly.

My older brother and I are close—or, we were before he was traded and moved from Chicago, where we've both lived our entire lives, to Las Vegas to play for the Vegas Aces last year. His fiancée, Nicki, is one of my best friends, and they're getting married this weekend. I'm the maid of honor, and they're flying me out Thursday for the bachelorette party before all the wedding festivities begin.

Work obligations have kept me from visiting very often since they moved there. In fact, I've only been out once, and it was just for a quick weekend. We hit a nightclub on the Strip and drank too much, but mostly we hung out at their house since they'd just moved in and I offered to help with the unpacking.

I never really considered actually moving to Vegas, but the idea of starting fresh has a nice ring to it.

"I don't have a job there," I say.

"Well, not to be the dick reminding you of this, but you don't have a job in Chicago, either," he counters.

"Ouch. Okay, fine, but I don't know anybody there." I already know this is a losing argument. If Todd was right about me badgering people about things until I get my way, well, it's because I learned it from Josh.

"You know Nicki. You have me. And you know that if we're both in the same city, Mom and Jimbo will eventually come too."

I roll my eyes. He always calls our dad, whose name is Jim, *Jimbo*. "Ah, the ulterior motive unmasked. You want Mom and Dad close by so when you and Nicki start shitting out babies, you have sitters nearby."

"Well, let's start with A, that's a disgusting way of putting it. B, we have no child plans on the current radar. I just miss having you all within a few miles, that's all."

I blow out a breath. He's being vulnerable, and it's starting to soften me. "I don't have anywhere to live." He starts to say something, but I interrupt. "And before you get any crazy ideas, I'm not living with you and Nicki. Living with newlyweds sounds frickin' awful, and I also don't want to stay alone in your huge-ass mansion while the two of you are off on your honeymoon. I'm almost positive it's haunted."

He laughs. "We're having some renovations done while we're out of town so you wouldn't want to stay here anyway. I have a good buddy who you can stay with until you find somewhere permanent. He's on the team, and he's a real stand-up kind of guy. He's got this huge house so you wouldn't really even have to see him, and it isn't haunted. The best part is that he lives across the street from me, so you won't actually be in the newlywed's house, but you'll be close. No flirting, though. He's recently single and not looking."

"Ha," I say without actually laughing the word. "Same here. No worries, I'm not in the market right now either. Unless he wants a fling. And he's hot. Then maybe. Is he hot?"

"Gross, Elle. God, you've always been so damn boy crazy. No hooking up with my friends."

This time I do laugh. "Okay, okay."

"You'll do it?" he asks.

"Do I really have a choice? Live in a mansion with your hot friend in a tropical paradise with mountains, palm trees, slot machines, and new opportunities…or stay here in Chicago where we haven't seen the sun in the last twenty-one days and I just got dumped and lost my job in the same damn day?"

"He's not *hot*," Josh argues, but he's missing the point.

I laugh. "What the hell. It's worth a shot, and if it doesn't work out, I can just come back home."

I can hear his smile in his voice. "Yes! We'll have so much fun. I'll introduce you to all the guys on the team, and you and Nicki can hang by our pool all day. She's missed you so much. And we'll find you a job in public relations out here. I've got tons of connections and you know I'll do anything to help."

"I know you will. I love you, big bro."

"Love you, too, little sis."

We hang up, and I get moving. I've got some packing to do, and it's not all going to fit in the one little suitcase I just pulled down from my closet shelf.

I call my mom next. My mom and I are close, but she tends to err on the side of critical, and while most often I just brush it off as something my mom does, sometimes it digs in a little deeper. "Josh just talked me into moving to Vegas," I blurt when she answers.

"What?" she gasps, and I laugh.

"Well, it's kind of a long story," and one you don't tell your mom, "but today I was fired and Todd and I broke up."

I pause just long enough to hear her mutter something about how she's going to have to wait even longer for grandchildren now, and I rush ahead with my speech.

"Josh told me to come live there while I get back on my feet, and I don't really see a reason not to." Except all the ones I named when Josh first brought it up, but admitting all that wouldn't exactly sell this idea to my mother.

"So you're just...leaving?" she asks, and I can tell she's totally flabbergasted but it's my life and I'm at the point where I need to stop living it as a way to please my parents.

"Yep. Oh, and can I leave my furniture in your basement for a while until I decide if I'm staying there or coming back?" I ask.

Okay, I don't *ask*. I plead.

"Of course you can, Ellie, but are you sure about all this?" Her tone is doubtful. "Aren't you sort of making a snap decision here?"

"Absolutely," I admit. "But what's the worst thing that could happen?"

What's the worst indeed.

By the time I'm boarding the plane to Vegas two days later, my brother has arranged for movers to pick up my essentials and move the rest of my furniture to my parents' place. Thank goodness for that fat pro-football paycheck and a generous big brother, am I right?

I said my goodbyes to my parents, which weren't really goodbyes as much as they were *see you tomorrow* since they're heading to Vegas for Josh's wedding too.

I said my goodbyes to my friends, but let's be honest. Everyone I was *really* close to either scattered after college or was left behind when I was fired from my job. Even Brittany, the girl who I would consider my best friend at the office, pretty much abandoned me over the last few days, citing an overwhelming amount of work since two people on the team were fired in the same day.

Okay, so maybe it's a little my fault she's overworked right now...but I could still use a friend.

The only close friend I have left is Nicki, who is engaged to my brother. I'll finally have the sister I always wanted, and I found her in someone who has been like a sister to me since we were in high school.

I'm ready for this move. It feels right even though it's a little scary. At least I'll have my brother, which means I'll also have all the Vegas Aces football players he's close to. They're a tight-knit bunch, a real family according to Josh, and he assured me over and over that I'll be included in that equation, too.

And I'm not just ready for the move. I'm also ready to meet the hot stud of my dreams...but just for a little fun. I did just get dumped by Todd, and I don't know how permanent this move is going to be.

When the wheels touch down and I look out the window to see the famed skyline of Las Vegas Boulevard, something pulls in my stomach as dreams and magic collide with that feeling of *home* for the first time in my life. I love this city. I've loved it every time I've visited, and it's not just the bright, flashing lights or the neon signs or the excitement of the Strip. It's not just the beautiful weather or the gorgeous scenery. It's a feeling, some inexplicable thing inside me that I want to keep experiencing over and over again.

My head keeps telling me this isn't a permanent move, but I think my heart just might have other plans.

CHAPTER 3

"Ahh, you're getting married in two days!" I yell when I see my brother. He grabs me up in a big hug, and we both laugh.

"Is that Josh Nolan?" someone nearby says as they pass us.

My brother lets me go and smiles at the passerby. "It is," he says. "Pleasure to meet you." He sticks out his hand and the guy shakes it vigorously.

"We're huge Aces fans," he says. "That pass you caught in the third quarter in that last game was inhuman."

Josh laughs, and I just stand by as I smile awkwardly. It *was* a great catch, but they ended up losing the game, so the Aces technically finished in third last season. They didn't make it to the Super Bowl, but they have high hopes that they will this year.

And I need to be honest for a second.

I literally know next to *nothing* about football.

I'm just repeating shit my dad said.

The quarterback passes the ball and they run into the end zone. Someone kicks a ball and they can score points that way too. They wear lots of padding because it's a violent game and they wear tight pants that look better on some players than others.

That's about the extent of my knowledge.

I watch all Josh's games, of course. I'm a supportive sister. But I'm not really paying attention to the *game*. I'm watching the fans in the stands go crazy for their team. I enjoy the fanfare even if I don't really understand it. My dad has tried to explain it to me hundreds of times, but usually I tune out.

I'm still a huge Aces fan, though. In fact, I'm wearing my favorite women's Nolan 18 jersey, in part because it's my own last name and in part because it's my brother's jersey and in part because I'm here in Vegas and it's fun when people start chatting me up about how great the team did last season.

I think I've heard *worst to almost first* at least a dozen times since I got to the airport this morning in my jersey. It was the Aces' tagline last season after a dismal performance the season before. They brought in a ton of fresh blood and a whole new coaching staff, and suddenly they're a top contender to head to the big game next year.

The fan chats him up a while longer, we grab my suitcases, and he leads me out to his boat of a car, a Nissan Armada—something he claims he needs because of his height and bulkiness.

"So what's the plan?" I ask once I'm buckled in.

"Nicki's getting ready now so she can just go to the hotel with you." He maneuvers out of the parking deck and toward the exit. "You can borrow one of my cars, and you'll go check in, party it up, watch my girl so she doesn't get too wasted, and then tomorrow we'll have breakfast with Mom and Dad, the men will go golfing, and then we'll have the rehearsal dinner."

"Are you ready for all this?" I ask.

One side of his mouth lifts as he glances over at me. "I've been ready to marry that girl since the day I told her I had feelings for her. Maybe even before that."

"When does football start back up?" I ask after he's paid for his short term in the parking deck.

"I have to report back for training camp at the end of July," he says. He signals a lane change and then we're off toward his mansion. "So we've got the wedding, then a few days later we leave for three weeks in Fiji, and then a little over a month to enjoy married life."

"You liking it out here?" I'm partly asking as a way to check up on my brother, but I'm partly asking because I genuinely want to know if he likes it. If he's happy. If *I* will like it.

"I fucking love it, Ellie," he says, and then he begins this impassioned speech like I've never heard out of him. "The weather, the palm trees, the blackjack tables, the food, the entertainment. It's all incredible. Unbeatable. But most of all, I love the Aces. I loved playing for the Bears, too. They're our hometown team. But this new coaching staff at the Aces is incredible. They've managed to bring us together in a way where every single guy on the team is a brother to me. In fact, I don't know if I told you this, but one of the guys who has been on the team longer than me is my best man."

I raise a brow. As maid of honor, that'll be the guy escorting me. "So I'll be walking down the aisle with a football friend?"

He nods. "Not just a friend. My best friend. And, incidentally, the guy you'll be living with since you refuse to live with me. So be nice to him."

I laugh. "I'm always nice. Maybe you should tell him that, too."

"Oh, don't worry. He's been fully warned about you."

I narrow my eyes at my brother in a *what the hell is that supposed to mean* kind of way, but he just laughs.

He pulls into his four-car garage that's actually a six-car garage with the lifts he has in there. He's a car guy. I am not. "Which one do you want to borrow?"

I glance over at the collection. I'll be driving one of these cars down Las Vegas Boulevard, and that's more than a little daunting. "Which one's the least expensive in case I wreck it?"

He laughs. "Don't wreck it. The Mercedes is probably the closest to your style."

"Do you mean because of my little Camry?"

He lifts a shoulder. "I just mean a sedan. It's yours while you're here. Except seriously, Elle." He shortens my name by a syllable. "Don't wreck it."

We're both laughing as we walk into the house, through an expansive laundry room, and into the even more expansive kitchen that's something right out of an architectural magazine. Or a kitchen magazine. Some magazine. "This place is ridiculous," I mutter.

"You're here!" Nicki yells as she walks into the room. She looks like she just stepped off the pages of some other kind of magazine with her long, blonde hair cascading in perfect waves down her shoulders and a cute white romper that would look totally ridiculous on me.

"Oh my God, it's the bride!" I gush, and she giggles as she beelines for me and grabs me into a hug. "Happy wedding weekend."

She squeezes me tight. "Thank you. I'm so happy you're here. Now let's get to the hotel and get the party started."

I laugh, but we don't waste time. She already has her little overnight bag packed with make-up and hair supplies, the dress she's planning to wear is in a wardrobe bag, and she has another bag filled with liquor. "Ready?"

Josh puts everything in the Mercedes, including my suitcases, and then we're off for the Cosmopolitan. It's only a twenty-minute drive, but it's filled with excited chatter not just for the night ahead but the entire weekend.

I'm at the check-in desk and Nicki is at the clerk beside me checking in when my clerk says, "Okay, Miss Nolan, we have you in one of our wraparound terrace suites for three nights. Is that correct?"

"Well, yeah, the three nights thing is correct," I say, a little confused. "I'm checking out Sunday. But did you say a suite?"

"Yes, ma'am," the clerk replies. "The reservation here requests a suite."

Nicki elbows me. "Just take it. It's the least we could do for our maid of honor."

I narrow my eyes at her, and I'm about to put up a complaint when I stop. If they want to treat me to a suite, who am I to take that away from them? I nod. "Thank you," I murmur, and she smiles.

"We got the penthouse, so don't thank me until you make the comparisons."

I laugh, and then we're on our way to wait for our luggage and get ready for our night out. The penthouse is where she'll get ready for her wedding on Saturday, and it's also where she'll be spending the night for the next few nights—tonight after the bachelorette party, tomorrow after the rehearsal dinner, and Saturday after the wedding.

She comes with me to my room first, and after my suitcase arrives, I grab the dress I'm wearing tonight and we head up to her room, where we'll get ready for our night out.

And then the fun begins.

CHAPTER 4

I haven't had a strawberry daquiri since I was in high school, and I think I'm getting brain freeze.

It's preventing me from actually getting drunk, if I'm being totally honest. The frozen concoction is slowing the intake, but Nicki treated us all to those dumb yard drinks that are a pain in the ass to carry around. She's all classed up with a tiara that has penises hanging off it, and it's our job to do what she says tonight. She and I lead the pack as we walk through a mall to get to the restaurant she chose for dinner, and her six other bridesmaids trail along behind us.

Nicki worked in finance when she lived in Chicago, but when they made the move to Vegas, she started doing charity work with the wives of some of Josh's teammates. The bridal party is a mix of friends from Illinois and the friends she's made out here, and so far, everyone seems to be getting along well.

Thankfully the restaurant doesn't allow the yard drinks, so we all ditch them in a garbage can out front before we head in to eat. Since I started with rum in my daquiri, I order a mojito.

It goes down fast.

I order another.

Now I'm starting to feel it, that tipsy feeling where everything is funny and I don't feel sick just yet. I luxuriate there a while as we wait for our dinners, listening to the conversations around me. Some of the ladies are talking about what it's like being a football wife, giving Nicki advice about how to maintain her own identity and still support her husband. A woman named Leah says, "Yep, you need to lift your husband up or else you'll end up single and some woman half his age will swoop in on him."

"Oh my God, that reminds me! Ellie, tell the story of how you just ended up single," Nicki demands out of the blue.

My eyes edge over to her. "Uh...what?" I was actually sort of content just listening in on the other stories.

"Tell them what happened," she urges me, and I sigh.

"I lost my job and my boyfriend," I mutter. And then I look up at all the women whose eyes are fixed on me. I let out a laugh. "On the same day."

Once I laugh, it seems like that's the go-ahead for everyone else at the table, too, so I continue.

"It was just this past Tuesday!" I say, and okay maybe I'm a little more than *tipsy* because I start laughing so hard at that I have to actually wipe tears from my eyes.

At least they're tears of laughter. I haven't shed any *real* tears over Todd...though I do miss the sex. And my job.

"What happened?" Krista, one of the football wives, asks.

"Well, we were, you know, *getting busy* in his office and our boss walked in." I air quote *getting busy* and my face would probably be burning with embarrassment if I wasn't a few mojitos deep and this wasn't a bachelorette party where these sorts of stories are pretty run of the mill. I mean, for God's sake, Nicki's wearing a dick-shaped necklace that matches her tiara.

"She fired us both, and he blamed me and dumped me on the spot."

"Oh, Ellie, that's awful," Jen, a girl Nicki and I went to college with, says.

I lift a shoulder. "Eh, Todd was good in bed but I never really saw him as part of my forever story. For a while I thought maybe he was my Prince Charming, but he turned out to be just another frog."

"We need to get this girl laid tonight!" Nadine, another football wife, says.

I giggle and hold up a hand. "It's fine. I'm fine. Everything's fine."

Everyone at the table laughs, and then Nicki says, "Bridal mission one. Get the maid of honor laid. Hey, maybe we'll find someone for you at the Man Mansion we're heading to next."

"Yeah, hook me up with a male stripper," I say, my voice dripping with sarcasm. "Because what happens in Vegas stays in Vegas."

"Except STDs," Jen sings, and everyone laughs. Then she asks, "While we're on the topic, who here has had a one-night stand?"

"Oh wait!" Nicki says. "Before you answer, let's make it a game!" She glances around the table. "Okay, everyone has a drink. Let's play *I Never*. I will start, and if you've done it, you have to take a drink. We'll go around the table until our food gets here."

I haven't played a drinking game since...okay, since last weekend when Todd and I watched a movie and drank every time the main character said *fuck*, but still.

Nicki looks giddy, and it's such a stupid, immature game, but we're here for the bride. "I never had sex outdoors." She takes a sip of her drink, and I shoot her a look that says *gross* since I'm sure she's talking about her sex life with my brother.

I take a sip. I've had my fair share of outdoor sex. Everyone else at the table drinks, too.

"I'll go next," Jen says. "I never had sex in water."

Everyone drinks, and Nicki looks at Nadine next.

"I never had sex with a pro football player."

Nadine, Krista, Leah, and Nicki all drink, and the rest of us all look at them with a touch of jealousy. Maybe now that I'm here in Vegas, Josh can introduce me to some of his hot football friends and next time I play *I Never*, I can drink to that question.

"Ellie, you go," Nicki says.

"Okay, I never had a one-night stand," I admit, and I don't touch my glass.

Every other woman at the table takes a drink.

Including Nicki, who has been with my brother for the last seven years and who has been my best friend since high school...but I already knew about her one night. She was seventeen and a virgin, and it was the summer before we left for college. She wanted to get it over with, and she never talked to the guy again. She also has zero regrets about that.

"Seriously?" I yell. "I'm the *only* one who hasn't?"

The women all laugh, but it's Delia, one of Nicki's old work friends, who speaks up first. "Mine was on my twenty-first birthday and I just wanted to have some fun."

"Mine was after a work happy hour and it was really awkward when we ran into each other the next day at the office," Brianna, another former work friend of Nicki's, says.

Each woman tells her story. It was in a corner of a nightclub. It was a Tinder date. It was on a vacation. Some are happier with the outcome than the others.

"And after tonight, you'll be able to tell your story about your one night with a male stripper," Nicki says.

"Oh please," I mutter. "Like I'm going to bang a stripper. Maybe a hot guy at the club afterward, though..."

Our dinners arrive, and we barely even got the game off the ground.

But now that this one-night stand idea is in my head, I can't pretend like it doesn't sound like one hell of a good time.

After dinner, we head to the strip club, where we stick dollar bills in thongs, yell and scream uncontrollably, and drink some more.

I most definitely don't hook up with a stripper, though I can't deny some of them are *hot*. But the oil…there's a lot of oil. Like *a lot*. I think I'd just slide right off some of them.

Laughter is rampant as the eight of us pile into a car to head back to the hotel, where we'll go to the nightclub and dance before we officially call it a night. Nadine and Leah bow out as soon as we get back to the hotel, and Krista heads out with them since they're her ride.

But Jen, Delia, and Brianna are all here in town visiting from Chicago, and they're all staying at this hotel. They're here for a good time just like I am, and we're here to shower our bride to be with attention, drinks, and dancing.

We head into Marquee Nightclub, where the music pounds and drinks are quite a bit more expensive than the restaurant—but, according to Nicki who is now slurring, "It's all good because Josh is footing the bill."

And speaking of my brother, we've only been dancing for what seems like five minutes when he saunters up behind Nicki and laces his arms around her waist. He says something in her ear, and she giggles, and I look away because this might be my best friend, but it's also my *brother*. He must've ended his bachelor party at the same club as us, and clearly those two drunken lovebirds will shortly be heading up to the penthouse to use that suite to their advantage.

A second later, they're making out, and I just keep dancing with Jen, Delia, and Brianna, and then it's time to break the seal, so to speak.

Jen comes with me to the bathroom because of that unspoken rule that girls don't use the restroom alone, and as we're walking down the hallway back toward the dance floor, she asks, "Find anyone for that one-night stand yet?"

I hear some guy say, "I volunteer!"

I shoot Jen a look and the two of us laugh as we practically run back to our friends. When we get back, though, two of those friends are gone. Josh and Nicki must've headed up to their room, and Delia and Brianna seem to have found some boys to talk to.

I look at Jen. "Another drink? Or head up to bed?"

"Another drink," she says, and we head to the bar. We order and wait.

"Let's not forget the bride's orders that I'm the sole woman left with the mission to find you a guy to sleep with," she says. She's kind of drunk, and even with the loud music, she's still loud. I was pretty drunk at the strip club, but all the dancing has driven me back from drunk to tipsy.

"I'm gonna need another drink for that," I say.

"Did she really just say she wants to find you a guy to sleep with?" someone to my left asks.

I shiver. The voice is deep and husky and too close to my ear, tickling me and somehow turning me on at the same time. I should turn and slap the guy, but I don't.

Because I'm just tipsy enough that sleeping with a guy just to earn my one-night stand banner still sounds like fun.

And when my eyes meet his...

Holy. Shit.

This is most definitely my candidate.

CHAPTER 5

A ripple of desire travels all the way down my spine and back up again.

His eyes are a dark blue and hold an air of mystery. I don't know if I've ever found bone structure sexy before, but man, this guy's is one hundred percent perfect. He looks like he might be fake, maybe a sculpture or a painting—you can't be that hot and be *real*—but the little bit of scruff on his jaw makes him human again. He's got these lips that I want to drown in and this magnificent, short hair I want to run my fingers through and the actual physical attraction I have the moment I see him is a crazy tangible thing.

He wears a white t-shirt and jeans, and it's so simple yet so ridiculously hot. The shirt stretches across a broad chest with muscled biceps peeking out the sleeves.

I want those arms wrapped around my body. I want those lips on mine. I want to see the goods hidden beneath the shirt and jeans.

I can't help it when I sigh with lust and an ache pulses between my legs.

If ever there was a candidate for a one-night stand based solely on looks alone, I'd tag this guy in a heartbeat.

"Why?" I ask, somehow keeping my cool despite the fact that I'm talking to hands down the hottest guy I've ever seen in my life. And then I say something stupid. "You volunteering?"

My eyes widen after the words slip out. He laughs, and it's this musical sound that I want to hear again and again. I want to record it and make it my ringtone. Is that weird?

"No," he says, and I'm filled with disappointment.

Wait a second.

I'm filled with disappointment?

I don't even know this guy, and I'm disappointed that he's not volunteering to sleep with me tonight?

"Well, not yet, anyway," he clarifies. "I like to at least get to know a girl's name before I sleep with her. And maybe hit her with a bad pick-up line."

I laugh as the disappointment dissipates. And then I basically let him know I'm game for sex by telling him my name since that's one of his two prerequisites for sleeping with a stranger. "Ellie," I say.

"Nice to meet you, Ellie. I'm Luke."

"Go ahead and hit me with the bad line." I can't help the twinkle in my eye as I wait for it.

He grins. "Hey good lookin'. You come here often?"

I giggle. "That's pretty bad."

Hot Luke waves to the bartender when he sets the drinks in front of us to indicate that he'll treat.

"You don't have to do that," I say. I'm about to tell him my brother is rich and he's paying for my drinks, but I stop myself.

"I want to," he says.

"Why?" I ask.

He shrugs. "I don't know. I'm not usually the guy who buys random women drinks at nightclubs. I'm not even the guy who *goes* to nightclubs."

"And yet you're here," I point out. "And, for the record, I'm not the girl who accepts drinks from strangers. I'm not even from Vegas."

He laughs. "So what are you doing here?"

"You know, my entire life has turned upside down in the last few days, and I guess I'm turning over a new leaf."

Hot Luke lifts his glass to mine. "I'm working on some new leaves, too. Let's get drunk and see where the night takes us."

I clink my glass against his, and I spot a hint of sexy danger in his eyes. "Getting drunk with you probably isn't my smartest move."

I turn and look at Jen, who shrugs. "He's hot, Ellie. Go for it."

I laugh. "You're a big help."

She holds up both hands. "Hey, my mission is complete. Now it's up to you."

"What was her mission?" Hot Luke asks.

"I'll tell you, but only after we dance and drink and then find a quiet place to talk that isn't a hotel room so you can prove you're not a bad guy."

"Whoa," he says. "That's a lot of pressure. But I think I'm up to the task."

I laugh. "We'll see, Hot Luke."

"Hot Luke?" he asks.

I smile a little sheepishly. "Sorry. That's what I heard in my head when you said your name, and clearly that's how I will reference you when I talk about this night from now until the end of time."

He laughs, and his genuine smile makes him even hotter. "Okay, then, Sexy Ellie. Let's dance."

I glance at Jen, who gives me the *go on, shoo* signal, and I head with Hot Luke to the dance floor.

We start out a little awkwardly, but it only takes about the length of one song before we get comfortable with one another.

He moves in a little closer.

I fling an arm around his neck.

His fingers dig into my hip.

I grind on his leg.

We dance, and we talk, and we laugh, and we dance some more. We throw inhibitions out the window thanks to our drinks.

He's got moves.

"I read once that the way a person dances is the way they bone," he says after we get drink refills and we're heading back to dance some more.

"Bone?" I tease.

He laughs. "Yeah. What do you call it?"

"Bang."

"Okay, so the way a person dances is the way they *bang*. I'll forever use that word now instead of *bone*."

I giggle at the lasting impact I'll clearly have on Hot Luke. "Deal. And where are you going with this fun fact?"

"I took dance lessons."

I laugh. "Did you take sex lessons, too?"

He shakes his head and shoots me maybe the slyest smile anyone has ever shot anybody before. "Don't need lessons for that when you start out at expert level."

I'm getting closer and closer to the point where I'm ready to find out if that's true.

I'm hot, and I'm thirsty, and, above all else, I'm freaking *horny* for this guy. I know I met him literally a half hour ago, but let's call a spade a spade. I want a one-night stand, and it's not like those are all about finding some deep connection with another person.

It's about attraction, lust, and animal instincts, and all three are on-fucking-point for me at the moment.

We dance a few more songs when he nods toward the door. "Let's get out of here and find somewhere to get to know each other," he suggests, and I nod even though I don't know if he means get to know each other or *get to know each other*. Like, literally? Or, you know, in the carnal sense?

I follow him out of the club and through the hotel, and we end up near one of the hotel's three pools. One of the other pools here turns into a nightclub on the weekends, and that's the one Josh and Nicki reserved to hold their wedding the night after tomorrow.

He settles onto a lounge chair, stretching his long legs out in front of him, and I take a beat to really look at him. He's glowing blue from the pool lights, but he's still definitely the hottest guy I've ever seen in my life.

Why is he talking to *me*? He could have any girl in that place.

And then a dart of reality hits me. Right. My friend screamed about how she wanted to find a guy I could have sex with, and Hot Luke was the one who overheard. He thinks I'm a sure bet, and even though I'm still pretty tipsy, that thought leaves me a little hollow.

I haven't had a one-night stand before because sex means something important to me.

But just for tonight...maybe I need to let that go.

When else am I ever going to have the chance to sleep with someone who looks like Hot Luke?

The answer is *never*.

I force myself to get out of my own head and enjoy this time. I slide onto the chair next to Luke's and lean back.

Jeez, this chair is comfortable. It's padded and sturdy and I could freaking sleep out here.

It's quiet down here near the main pool, but Vegas is never *really* quiet. The bass from some speakers not too far away pounds, and I feel the beat in my chest. There aren't any people here, though, where the club was pulsing with the constant hum of bodies. Out here, it's just the two of us, and between the shadows moving with the water and the relative quiet, the setting provides an almost romantic tranquility.

"God, I hate nightclubs," he mutters as he rubs his temples, and I laugh.

"Why were you at one, then?"

He flashes me a grin, and butterflies start battering around in my stomach. "Because of fate." When I roll my eyes with a laugh, he admits, "I went for a buddy."

"I don't like them, either," I say, thanking God for the tipsiness that allows me to talk to someone who has a smile like that. "I'm more of a *grab a few drinks at a bar with friends* kind of girl. I guess I liked them more when I was younger."

"So why were you there?"

"I went for my best friend." I leave it at that instead of getting into the whole bachelorette party thing, which will get into the reason why I'm here, which will lead to the wedding and the fact that my brother plays professionally and it's all just details I don't want to share.

I want this stranger all to myself.

"Ah, something in common," he says, nodding sagely. "That's surely the way to prove I'm not a bad guy."

I laugh. "We're getting there. Are you single?" I ask it because I feel like you should know these details about your one-night conquest.

He spits out the fewest possible details. "I broke up with a long-term girlfriend a few months ago."

"Why?" I ask.

He sighs. "We were together a little over a year when she moved in. And then I realized there was no future for us."

My brows dip down. "Why?"

"She would put sugar in her coffee, stir the coffee, and then leave the used, wet spoon in the jar of sugar."

I laugh. "That's an interesting reason to dump somebody."

"There were little clumps of cold coffee sugar all the time. I even made a jar of sugar that was just for her. But that was sort of the tipping point where I started to notice everything else that made us completely incompatible, you know?"

I nod. "What else?"

He shrugs. "She didn't brush her teeth until bedtime some days. She was a mess in the bathroom, make-up and hair shit everywhere. Oh, plus she was manipulative as fuck."

"She sounds awful."

He chuckles. "Yeah, she pretty much was."

I glance over at him. "Are you over her?"

"Yeah. It had been over a long time. You know?" He shrugs. "My buddies tonight told me I need to get laid. I just guess I'm not ready to jump back into something after the mess my last relationship turned out to be." He's quiet for a beat, and then he says, "Your turn for the hot seat. Why are your friends trying to get you laid?"

"Apparently I'm the only one of them who hasn't had a one-night stand," I admit.

"I could definitely help you out there now that I know your name."

I giggle. "Oh, and I should probably also tell you, this past Tuesday, I was dumped and lost my job on the same day."

He sits up and swings his legs so he's facing me. He leans forward with his elbows on his knees and clasps his hands in front of him. "Now this is a story I want to hear." His eyes twinkle. They *glow* at me, actually, and I get a little lost in them for a beat.

I know this is only meant to last one night, but for just a second, I think there could be more with someone like him. I realize I'm not ready for all that after starting fresh in a new city, but my chest aches for a second as the connection we seem to share plows into me.

I twist my lips and debate how honest to be, and then I go for it. Hell, everyone else knows the story by now. I may as well be honest with a stranger. "I seduced the guy I was seeing while we were in his office and our boss caught us."

"Oh God, that had to be awkward."

"It gets worse. I was just about to, you know..." I trail off, and he looks confused, so I spell it out even though my cheeks are burning with embarrassment. "Orgasm. I was about to orgasm when she walked in. And then he shifted when he heard the door, and it shot me over, and then I had an orgasm while my boss watched. And then she fired us both."

"At least tell me you had your clothes back on when she fired you." His voice holds just a hint of teasing, and I can't help my laugh.

"Yeah, I did. I was wearing a dress so I hadn't taken anything off. She gave us a minute to compose ourselves."

"Did he finish?" he asks, genuinely curious and invested in my story at this point.

I throw up both hands. "No! He didn't even want to!"

"That guy is fucking insane. He was banging a girl as hot as you in his office and he didn't even finish?"

I shrug nonchalantly but it doesn't escape my attention that he just called me *hot*.

Me.

Hot.

He thinks I'm hot.

That's right.

And he used my word.

"Good use of *bang*. And right?" I ask, somehow maintaining my cool as I let the word slide by. "So the boss comes back in, fires us both, leaves, and then he tells me something about how this isn't working for him."

"Ouch."

"It's fine," I say with the flip of a hand. "We'd only been casually dating a couple months. It's not like I was in love with him or anything."

"So you're over him, and I'm over my ex, and we're just two single people sitting by the pool and dancing around the fact that we want each other just for tonight while I try to prove to you that I'm not a bad guy."

I smirk. "I think you've proved it. You didn't even try to kiss me in the club, not even when I was practically humping your leg." Yeah, alcohol tends to make my filter disappear. I'd *never* say that to someone if I was totally sober. Particularly not to someone as gorgeous as this guy. I wouldn't have given him all those details about Todd if I was sober, either.

I mean, *probably* not, anyway. My brain to mouth filter has been known to malfunction upon (frequent) occasion.

We're quiet for a beat, and then he says in a voice so husky it's dripping with sex, "Oh, Sexy Ellie. I wanted to. I was just trying to prove I'm a good guy."

My chest swells and the ache between my thighs pulses.

"I wanted you to." My voice is low and it's a clear invitation.

He unclasps his hands and stands, and then he moves with caution toward my chair. I look up at him, and maybe he should look dangerous out here since he's a total stranger, but he doesn't. There's something intrinsic between the two of us that makes me trust him. I feel it deep in my bones. He's *not* a bad guy, and I want this. He wants this. We're two consenting adults.

I'm still stretched out on my chair, and he reaches down with both hands. I set my hands in his, and he pulls me up to standing.

Then he sits, and he pulls me back down so I'm straddling his lap. All memories of straddling Todd in a desk chair are easily replaced with this, the new memory I'll have of the hottest moment I ever straddled someone. He looks up at me, and I look down at him, and it isn't just the Vegas heat that's passing between us.

The sexual tension drips thickly all around us, too thick to cut with a knife. It's this palpable thing I can feel, and then he reaches a hand under my hair as he cups my neck with his big palm.

His eyes are still hot on mine, and I read all the lust that surely he must see reflected back at him. And then he pulls my neck down until our lips touch.

I move both hands to his jaw, at once out of passion and to hold his face and feel the roughness and remind myself that this moment is really happening.

His lips are firm and tender at the same time, and when he opens his mouth and his tongue brushes against mine, I lose all sense. From out of nowhere comes this sudden feeling like I need this kiss in order to breathe, like if it stops so will my oxygen.

His hand remains on my neck, big and warm, and his other holds me at my waist. His fingers dig into me there, like he wants to feel my skin but my dress is in the way—like he's trying to rein in the passion but he just can't.

His body is warm and hard beneath mine, and all this kiss is serving to do is make me want this one night with him more than anything in the world.

I shift my hips down, and he shifts his toward me, too.

He wants this. He wants *me*.

The brush of his tongue turns into something hotter and more intense, and even though it's just a kiss on a patio by a pool, it feels like so damn much more. It's melting me into a puddle of lust for this man, and the way he's kissing me back tells me he feels it, too.

I finally pull apart from his mouth. Our eyes meet, and his are hooded with lust.

God do I want him.

"Come up to my room with me," I murmur, mostly because it would be indecent to do the things with him that I want to do right here on this pool lounge chair even though it's deserted out here.

His lips are swollen as he nips another kiss to my mouth, and then he pulls back with a lazy smile. "Let's go."

CHAPTER 6

As soon as the elevator doors seal us into privacy, he backs me up into the wall with his hips. He pins me there and kisses me like he's starved, like he can't wait until we get to my room. He drives his hips toward me, and I can't wait, either.

Lust presses thrills all the way through me, starting at the tips of my toes and exploding, fuzzing my brain and muddying my senses. I hold onto his arms not because I'm caught in the moment of lust but because I *need* to. I need him to hold me up and balance me, because just his kiss is enough to bring me to my knees.

If he bangs anything like he kisses, well, I'm in for a real treat.

His fingers start trailing up my torso. They stop short of my breast, and my nipple tightens with need.

We practically jog down the hall once the elevator doors open, and of course since it's a wraparound terrace suite, it's at the far end of the hallway.

"Nice place," he says once I let us into my room, and then he kicks the door shut behind him.

A brief beat of awkwardness falls between us.

We're here in my room now, and it's time for the sex, and...shit. I don't have any condoms.

"Uh," I start. "I just realized that I don't have any condoms."

He chuckles, and then he reaches into his pocket and produces a handful.

My eyes widen, and I press my lips together and tilt my head as I try to think through the best response to the fact that the stranger I just invited to my hotel room to sleep with has a pocketful of condoms.

"I don't typically carry this many around," he protests before I even get a chance to say anything. "My buddies wanted me to get laid tonight and they kept throwing them at me during dinner. Jokes on them, though, since I actually need one."

I raise a brow and lift a shoulder. "Maybe two."

He grins, and it's that smile that absolutely kills me.

"So how does this work?" I ask stupidly. I want him to kiss me again, but I don't know him well enough to read his signals.

His brows dip down. He shoves the condoms back in his pocket, and then he makes a circle with a finger and a thumb on one hand and pokes a finger from his other hand through it. "Insert tab A into slot B."

I laugh and rest my hands on my hips.

"Do you really not know how it works?" he asks, his brows drawn together in confusion. "Weren't you fired *while* you were having sex?"

"I know how *sex* works," I say with a touch of exasperation. "I just don't know how one-night stands work."

"Pretty much the same as regular sex, I think."

"Have you had one before?" I ask.

He lifts a shoulder and has the grace to look a little sheepish. "Yeah."

"All right, then. Get over here and pop my one-night stand cherry."

He doesn't waste any time before he pounces. He practically rips my dress over my head and sends it flying in one direction, and I kick off my heels then reach for the bottom of his shirt.

I'm a little slower. A little more nuanced.

And it's like unwrapping the sexiest present I've ever received.

As I pull his shirt up, I reveal muscle after muscle after muscle and then a solid, expansive chest. I toss his shirt on the ground and stare at his physique. It's muscled. It's ridged. It's hard. It's glorious.

I may drool a little.

My eyes flick up to his, and he's watching me carefully. "I, uh, work out a lot."

I laugh. "It would appear so." I run a hand up and down my torso sort of like I'm one of those models on *The Price is Right* and I'm showing off the merchandise. "I do not."

His eyes flick to my chest, over my stomach, and to my panties. "You're gorgeous," he murmurs, and then he takes a step toward me, and another, and then he reaches for me and pulls me against him. His skin is smooth and warm as he crushes my body to his, and then his mouth crashes back down to mine. He flicks the snap on my bra and it falls open in the back. He runs his fingertips up my spine until they tangle up into my hair, and my chest lights with anticipation.

He moves back and I shimmy out of my bra, and then he slides my panties down my legs. He moves slowly, and he runs his tongue along the inside of my thigh as he does it.

I shiver.

He pushes me back until my knees hit the bed, and I sit. He kneels between my legs and looks up at me for a beat, like he's checking whether it's okay to do as he pleases with me, and I offer a small smile through the lust. Looking down into his eyes when he's like this—his body lean and powerful, his eyes heavy—causes need to pulse through me. The ache between my legs grows nearly unbearable.

And then he dives in face-first. I grip the comforter with both hands as he licks his way through me, dipping his tongue inside before flattening it over my clit, and holy shit it feels so damn good. Pleasure courses through me as one carnal thought that I need this man inside me plagues my mind.

I mutter incoherent words of encouragement as my moans of pleasure fill the silence in the room. He adds a finger to what he's doing, and I grip onto his hair, that thick, luscious hair that I've wanted to touch since I first saw him. It's like his tongue was made to pleasure my body. The coil springs loose and I see a million fireworks and stars as I squeeze my eyes shut and my body flies into an intense, mind-blowing climax.

When it starts to slow and I realize I'm pulling on his hair, I let go. "Sorry," I murmur as I collapse back, my eyes closed as I try to recover from the high.

He laughs as I pant. I open one eye and see him still kneeling between my legs. He wipes his mouth with the back of his hand, and why the hell is that so damn sexy? Maybe because the back of his hand will smell like me now, like in some way I've marked my sex territory.

But he's not my territory—at least not beyond tonight. And that thought is somehow very freeing after everything that happened this week.

I want Hot Luke to slam into me from behind while I claw at the window. I want to do whatever he wants me to do so I can please him the way he just pleased me.

He's already made me come once, and he's still wearing his jeans.

That's just not okay.

So I sit up and tug his arms with the signal that he should stand. I'm eye-level with his stomach, and I lean forward and kiss that gorgeously ridged abdomen of his. Then I trail kisses down toward his jeans. I unbuckle his belt and pop the button. Before I reach in and see the goods, I rub my hand along the outside of his pants.

My heart races when I feel the thick steel hidden in there.

He doesn't make a sound, but when I glance up at him, his neck is corded and his head is tipped back as he relishes the feel of a woman touching him.

I lower his zipper and then I reach in. He groans as I pull him out, and then just like he dove face first into pleasuring me, I lick my way down his long shaft before I take him all the way to the back of my throat.

I pull back and then suck him back in, and his fingers tangle in my hair. When I repeat the motion again, this time he holds my head in place for a beat. A guttural growl rises out of his chest, and then he lets my head go.

Holy shit.

That was hot.

I lick up and down his shaft, and then he reaches under my arms and pulls me to standing.

We're eye to eye when he says, "If you keep doing that, I'm gonna lose it. If I lose it now, I won't get to fuck you."

His eyes are heated, and he leans forward to kiss me before he lets me go. He kicks off his shoes and pulls his jeans and boxers off, and I take in his fully naked body for a beat.

It's perfect.

Gorgeous.

Stunning.

Something from a dream.

And it's the first time I feel like it's too damn bad this is just one night. But that's all it is. Sex with a stranger. My one-night stand with the hottest guy I've ever seen in my life.

The girls will be so proud of me tomorrow when I get the chance to brag about my conquest.

We're definitely on the same page because after he rolls on one of the thirty condoms he pulled out of his pocket, he walks me over to the window. "Bend forward and use the glass to brace yourself," he says, his voice husky.

I do what he says, and I feel him close behind me. He swipes his dick through my slit before he shoves himself inside me. My body expands and adjusts to his size, and I don't know if I've ever felt so full...or so horny.

I claw at the glass as he starts moving. My hotel room is on a pretty high floor, but I see traffic as it's jammed on a Thursday night down on the Strip. People move about their night like everything's normal while I'm getting fucked from behind in a hotel room by a stranger.

I groan when he hits a particularly hot rhythm with me. When I glance up, I see his eyes hot on mine in the reflection of the glass.

The very best part of doing it like this is seeing his face as he does what he's doing to me from behind.

He holds my gaze, grunts and groans filling the room as I listen to the sounds of sex and his body slapping against mine.

Between the sounds and his eyes and the heat between us as he pleasures me in a way no man has ever managed to before, I feel the start of another orgasm edging its way toward me. I squeeze my eyes shut.

"Open your eyes," he demands, and I do.

He leans forward, his eyes on mine the whole time, and he reaches around to brush my clit with his fingertips.

And that's when I lose it completely.

I thrash around as I come, my body squeezing him inside as it contracts and pulses all around him, but I keep my eyes on him the whole time. His hot face screws up as he watches me, and then he picks up the pace, shoving hard into me with little growls that tell me he's right there with me.

He mutters a curse as he comes, and when his body starts to relax, he pulls out of me. My body immediately misses his, and even though he's already satisfied the ache twice, I feel it pulsing again. I want him again. I want *more*.

He helps me straighten to a stand, and we both pant for a beat before he sweeps me literally off my feet and into his arms. He kisses me as he carries me over to the bed, and it would potentially be the most romantic moment of my life if this was more than just a one-night thing.

He gets rid of the condom then collapses beside me as we attempt to recover from what was definitely the hottest few moments of my life.

I catch my breath and take a beat to breathe him in. I memorize the scent—it's fresh and clean and manly all at once, and I want to breathe it in forever.

I break the silence once I catch my breath. "Well that was..." I trail off as I try to find the right word. I fail.

"Hot," he finishes.

"Yeah. Hot."

He laughs, and he leans over and kisses the top of my head, and I giggle, and it feels like so much more of a *boyfriend* move than what this is.

I want to do it again, but the alcohol and the physical activity from tonight catch up with me. I'm about to drift into sleep when he mutters, "Shit. I have to go."

My eyes pop open, and a dart of sadness pulses through me. I push it away. "So soon?" I was hoping for another round or two before morning. I try not to think that it's *me* that's the reason why he's darting out so quickly.

He presses his lips together and nods as he clicks off his phone. I hadn't even realized he was looking at it since my eyes were closed. "I'm sorry. I have some stuff I need to take care of and an early morning."

He's clearly giving an excuse to get the hell out after we banged, and that's fine. We were both aware of the stakes going into it even though a huge part of me is disappointed and really, really wishes we could exchange numbers or at least Instagram handles, but that's not what this is supposed to be about.

We were destined to meet for one hot night, and now we've had it.

And that's that on that.

He gathers his clothes and I find a t-shirt and shorts to toss on while he dresses. And then with a heavy heart that makes me realize I'm just not cut out for these one-night deals, I walk him to the door, grabbing my phone on the way by. He kisses me once more at the door, and I swear my toes curl and my heart melts.

I snap a quick selfie of us before he can protest because obviously I need proof for the ladies that I spent the night with the hottest guy I've ever seen in my life—not at all because I want it for spank bank material.

Okay, maybe a little because I want it for spank bank material.

God, I could stare into those eyes for-damn-ever.

He presses his lips together in a sad smile. "Bye, Sexy Ellie. Thanks for the best one-night stand ever."

I brave a smile back. "Bye Hot Luke. Thanks for breaking my one-night stand cherry with the hottest sex of my life."

His sad smile widens to a grin, and then he opens the door and walks out of my life.

CHAPTER 7

"Why the hell would they do breakfast so damn early the morning after the bachelorette party?" I grumble to myself as I try to scrub away the gross feeling that seems to coat me from head to toe.

It's a little after eight, and Hot Luke left my room last night a little after two. My parents got into town on an early flight and headed right to Josh's place to make us all brunch, which is a lovely idea even though the timing sucks.

But we had to do it early-ish because Josh has a tee time with my dad and some of his groomsmen at eleven.

I slept like shit last night.

I don't think the gross feeling comes from my night with Luke, though maybe it should. I feel gross from the strip club, like maybe some oil dripped on me and I can't quite scrub it away. Or maybe it *is* Luke I feel gross over.

I don't really know how I'm supposed to feel the morning after a single night with a guy that was only about sex. But now I have the badge of honor, and I'll wear it proudly as I show off the selfie I've already stared at a billion times.

God, we're cute together.

My heart ripples every time I open my photos and see his gorgeous smile.

My chest tightens as I touch his face on the screen and recall the feel of the stubble lining his jaw as it scratched along my leg.

I had sex with that guy.

And I won't get to have it again.

That's the cost of the one-night thing, and I realize this morning that I'm not really cut out for that lifestyle. I want more. I want to see him again. I want to kiss him some more. I want to have sex with him again.

But I can't because all I really know about him is that his name is Hot Luke and he bangs like a sexpert.

And he busted out of there so fast after we banged that clearly he wasn't interested in anything else. To be fair, those were the parameters set forth when we met...but it still feels a little icky. He seemed like a good guy, but then he just ran out, and I don't really know how to feel about that other than a little sad.

I do my best to brush those feelings away. It was what it was, and it's over now.

After I try to scrub away all the feelings and fail, I get out of the shower. I have a missed text from Nicki.

Nicki: *I'm heading home with Josh this morning. Your parents are already there cooking. Meet us there when you get up. Thanks for the best night last night! Oh and bring me something if you stop at the Bux.*

I laugh. She knows I'll stop at Starbucks on my way—especially after a night like last night. I need the caffeine that fuels me in a way regular, homemade coffee just doesn't.

I search the area for a Starbucks on my app and find one close to my brother's house, and then I gather my wet hair in a ponytail, toss on a baseball cap since Nicki has hired in a team to get us ready for the rehearsal tonight, and head for valet to pick up my brother's car.

The Starbucks is only about fifteen minutes from the hotel, and Friday morning traffic in Vegas is relatively light. I'm battling a slight hangover and my body is still a little warm from what Luke did to it.

I sit in my car in the parking lot and place a mobile order on my app. I don't get my favorite nonfat white chocolate mocha with extra whip. I opt instead for one of the most caffeinated beverages on the menu—a nitro cold brew, which, according to my favorite barista back home, isn't the top most caffeinated drink on the menu, but the caffeine hits you quicker because of a little bit of carbonation. I punch in Nicki's favorite drink, a skinny latte, and I order a little something for Josh and my parents, too.

I stare at the picture of Hot Luke one more time for good measure, set it as my wallpaper because I'm totally going to play a joke on Nicki and tell her the guy is my new boyfriend, and then I get out of my car and head inside to pick up my drinks.

They aren't ready yet.

I stand by the counter to wait, and I slip my phone out of my pocket. I'm scrolling Instagram mindlessly, wondering if I should put up the picture of me with Hot Luke when I know I won't, when I hear a voice behind me.

A bragging voice.

At least it's low, but not low enough that I don't hear every word of his conversation. I'm the only one in hearing distance, and I probably look occupied as I scroll my phone.

"Oh, yeah, I banged her real good."

My brows dip down. What kind of asshole brags at the Starbucks mobile pickup area about the girl he had sex with last night?

"I spent all night screwing her brains out up against the window, and then I bolted."

His voice is still low, but I still hear it.

Up against the window?

My brains were screwed out up against a window last night.

And that voice…

It's low, but it's still deep and husky.

It's familiar.

But it can't be.

The heat of an arm brushes mine as someone beside me grabs a drink from the mobile pick-up area. I finally glance up from my phone.

The drink is labeled simply *Luke*.

Not *Hot Luke*, but when I look over and my eyes meet his, it's definitely Hot Luke.

He glances over at me like I'm in his way—or maybe it's to apologize for getting in *my* way—as he turns to leave, and when his eyes lock with mine, even beneath my baseball cap, I spot immediate recognition in his eyes.

And some regret...probably for the words he just said.

"I'll call you back." He hangs up his phone and slides it into his pocket, his wide, very confused eyes never leaving mine.

"Were you just *bragging* about last night?" I accuse at the same time he says, "What are you doing here?"

I don't have the energy to even answer him, so I set my hands on my hips and wait for his defense.

"I know that's how it sounded, but I swear to God, I'm not an asshole. He's just been badgering me to get laid, and I *know* I told you that last night, and he asked me if I hooked up, and I may have exaggerated a little for his benefit. Give me your number. I'll make it up to you, I promise."

He's rambling, and it would be cute if I didn't feel so...grossed out by his conversation.

I feel like I was a conquest that he could use to brag to his friends.

Granted, that's exactly what it was for me, too, so maybe I don't have a reason to be angry—especially since I was about to run to Nicki and tell her all about my night with a stranger...but somehow this taints what happened between us.

I wasn't about to brag every detail about my hands clawing the glass while he gave me the hottest orgasm of my life, but clearly he didn't leave the room with those same secrets.

"Order up for Ellie," the barista says, and she pushes a tray with four drinks plus another drink on the side across the counter.

I hold up a hand to Luke. "I'm good. Last night was..." I trail off.

"Hot?" he asks a little hopefully, repeating the same word he used just after we had sex.

I shake my head. "It was one night, and that's all." I pick up my five coffees. "One perfect night that I refuse to let you taint this morning. We weren't supposed to run into each other again, so I'm just going to pretend we didn't."

With those as my parting words, I spin on my heel and practically run out the door.

And just as I move in front of it to try to open it with one finger since my hands are full, someone on the other side pushes it open and right into me.

All five coffees tumble down to the ground.

I draw in a deep breath as I ward off the tears.

So *that* is how today's gonna go. Got it.

Hot Luke rushes over in some attempt to help me, but it's futile. The girl behind the counter yells, "Remake mobile order for Ellie!"

One of the workers rushes over with a mop and some paper towels from the back, and Luke picks up the five cups, and I stand there apologizing over and over and over as I blot at my shirt that will definitely smell like coffee for the rest of time.

Luke's eyes meet mine once the mess is cleaned. I press my lips together.

"You sure we can't at least exchange numbers?" he asks...*pleads*.

I shake my head. "Bye, Luke," I say, and then I turn toward the pick-up counter to wait for my remake.

Maybe he stares after me, or maybe not. I don't turn around to check as I sigh again. I can't deny that I felt a lot of things when I saw him. I can't help but wonder why he was at the same Starbucks as me at the same time. Serendipity, maybe? Fate? Or just a coincidence?

Whatever the case, he's gone when I finally do turn around. As I exit the store and carefully slide the drinks onto my passenger seat, I can't help but wonder what fate has in store and whether we'll run into each other again.

CHAPTER 8

I force myself to forget about Hot Luke and our Starbucks encounter as I pull into the driveway, and then I text Nicki to let her know I'm here since I won't have a free hand to ring the bell. I grab the five drinks and walk them up to the massive, imposing front door.

Nicki throws it open, and I go into immediate *Woo Girl* mode even though my heart most definitely isn't in it today. "Ahh! You're getting married tomorrow!"

You'd never guess she was drunk as hell last night based on her screaming reply: "Woo!"

I giggle, and she helps me with the drinks before I drop them *again*—probably since she knows that's totally my style.

"And how did your night end up?" she asks as she leads me into the house.

I giggle, and then I whisper (because my parents are two rooms away), "I did it."

Her head whips in my direction, and her eyes are wide. "You did what?"

"*It*," I whisper yell. "You know. A one-night stand."

"Oh my God!" she practically screams, and my parents are *definitely* going to want to know what that's all about. I motion with my hand that she really needs to take it down a notch, and she starts whisper yelling too. "With who? Holy shit, I'm so proud of you! What happened? How did you meet him? Did you exchange numbers?"

"I'll give you every detail later," I say as we walk through the house. I lower my voice to a whisper. "He was some random guy I met at the club. He was tall and had all these muscles and, ugh, he was just the hottest guy I think I've ever seen in my life. It was hot. No numbers, just one night." And then we're nearing the kitchen and I give her a look that clearly means we'll talk about it later because there's my dad, and hell if I'm going to brag about my one-night stand in front of my dad.

"There she is!" he says, and he steps over to wrap me in a hug while Nicki sets down the drinks. My mom is right behind him.

"Oh, honey, your eyes are all puffy," she says, and I roll those eyes for her benefit. "Did you drink a lot last night?"

No, mom, I got my brains screwed out up against a window and I was up kinda late after flying in yesterday and attending a bachelorette party. "Yeah," I say instead, which really isn't a lie.

She tuts disapprovingly. "Brunch is almost ready," she says, and she heads back to the stove to stir some scrambled eggs.

Can we really call it *brunch* when it's not even nine o'clock yet? Isn't that still in the breakfast zone? I guess it's almost eleven Chicago time, so I let it slide without saying anything—something I tend to do a lot around my mother.

We sit down to bacon, sausage, pancakes, and my mom's famous scrambled eggs, chatting about the wedding and today's activities. Josh and my dad leave for the golf course, and a short while later, the rest of the bridesmaids start to show up as well as Nicki's mom. Then a team of nail techs rings the bell and gets to work on us.

We're pampered with manicures and pedicures, with stylists who do our hair and make-up, and with racks of dresses to choose from.

By the time the boys get back from golf and take their showers, it's just about time to head back to the Cosmopolitan for the rehearsal.

I drive my brother's car back, valet it, and stop at my room to drop off my purse. I take a beat to look out the windows at the view. I spot a handprint on the window.

My handprint.

The terrace wraparound suite is just how it sounds. It's a corner room, and windows literally wrap around the entire suite, giving me a beautiful view of the Strip. I remember looking down over that view last night when Hot Luke was pounding into me, and a well of regret rises over me.

We could've exchanged numbers. Last names. Career details.

Okay, maybe not career details since at the moment I don't actually have one, but anything that would help identify the other.

I wish I could really pretend I never overheard his conversation at Starbucks this morning like I told him I would...but I can't. It replays in my mind, an endless loop where I wish I could see him again followed by rising anger that he spoke about me the way he did.

That he wrote me off so easily.

But I know he's been to that Starbucks at least once, so maybe when this weekend is all over, I'll go hang out there for a bit on the off chance I might run into him again. I sigh, and then I brush it off. I have to, because it's time to head toward the pool for the rehearsal.

A different pool than the one I sat near last night when Luke first kissed me, thank God.

I step on the elevator car, the same one I was in last night when I made out with Luke—back when there was the promise of sex in the air but we hadn't done anything more than some intense kissing.

I'm not alone, so I stare up at the digital numbers as they change with each passing floor as one does in crowded elevators.

I get off on the fourteenth floor and head toward the Chelsea Pool. I spot our small group standing near the entrance, and some of the groomsmen have joined us. I check them out from a distance as I approach. Tall, lean men with tight butts in suits. Mostly football players. Scratch that...mostly *hot* football players.

I wipe the corner of my mouth in case a little drool escaped as my eyes zero in on one with a particularly cute butt.

I don't know any of Josh's groomsmen. They're all his teammates on the Aces and I didn't meet any of them the one weekend I visited Nicki and Josh, but as he's told me over and over, they're like brothers to him after only a year of playing here.

He's talking to the small group of them, and after my one-night stand last night, I'm feeling a little overdose of confidence. It's not that I think I'm going to hook up with any of my brother's friends—not that I'm not opposed to the idea—but I have a little swagger to my walk just in knowing that someone as hot as Hot Luke wanted to spend some time in my bed.

Obviously that was purely about physical attraction.

Clearly he's an asshole who touts his conquests in public.

I shake it off and my confidence takes a little tumble as I trip when my heel stubs the sidewalk all at the same time. I don't fall, thankfully, but I do realize how much I have to let last night and subsequently also this morning go. I need to focus because when I don't, well, I trip and I drop coffees and it's usually a disaster.

"There she is," Josh says, looking over the shoulder of the super cute butt guy he's talking to. "My sister, the maid of honor," he announces, and he takes a step toward me to introduce me to the groomsmen.

The guy with the super cute butt turns around as Josh passes by on his way toward me.

My eyes flick from my brother to the guy in the suit.

No.

My eyes widen.

My heart stops.

It can't be.

My stomach twists.

It's just not possible.

My knees nearly give out on me.

"Ellie, this is my best man, Luke Dalton," Josh says.

Oh shit.

"Oh, and, by the way, he's the one who lives across the street from Nicki and me. He can't wait to have my little sister as his houseguest."

I swear to God, I'm the physical embodiment of the facepalm emoji.

You have got to be freaking kidding me.

CHAPTER 9

"Honey, you look pale. Do you feel all right?" my mom asks, walking over and pinching my cheeks to give me some color like she's done ever since I was a little girl.

Uh, no Mother, I actually *don't* feel all right. The guy who screwed my brains out against a window last night and was supposed to disappear without a trace is apparently not just my brother's best friend, but also in some crazy twist of fate...he's my new roommate.

I draw in a deep breath as I try to reconcile this new information. "I'm fine," I murmur, and Luke is definitely smirking and I want to slap that smirk right off his damn sexy face.

"Nice to meet you," I say to Luke, and I stick out my hand to shake his. His eyes find mine as he takes my hand. His grip is warm and firm. Just like other parts of him.

Of course Hot Luke is my brother's best man. Of-freaking-course he is. This is my life, so it just couldn't have happened any other way.

"You too," Luke says, playing the part just like I am. "Like your brother said, I'm happy to have you stay with me. Any little sister of Josh's is a little sister of mine." His words are thick.

He bangs my brother on the back, and some lightbulb clicks on in my brain. That's why he was at that club last night. My brother was there, too. I bet all the groomsmen were, but I didn't know any of them. I watch the games, but who the hell knows who's who under those helmets and when half of them are wearing those black stripes under their eyes?

Okay, fine.

I have the games *on*.

I don't really *watch* them.

I cheer when everybody else does. I boo when I hear others booing. But mostly I get work done on my phone while I pretend like I'm paying attention.

That's why I had no idea who Luke Dalton was when I bumped into him at the bar.

If I thought he was hot in jeans and a white t-shirt last night, well, he looks ridiculously re-fuckable in the suit today. And tomorrow in a tux? Forget about it.

Game over.

I don't know how the hell I'm going to survive this wedding weekend without giving in again.

And why shouldn't I give in again?

It was supposed to just be one night, but what if we were destined for more than that?

Oh God.

A horrible thought plagues me, and all the color drains from my face again.

When he was bragging on the phone...was he talking to *my brother*?

I feel like I might be sick.

"Now that everyone's here, allow me to introduce myself," some lady in a pantsuit says. "I'm Stella Porter." She pauses for dramatic effect like everyone should recognize the name. "I'm Nicole and Joshua's event coordinator, and tonight we're going to run through tomorrow's festivities."

Is *event coordinator* a fancy phrase for *wedding planner*?

I almost ask that question out loud, but I manage to stop myself.

"I need the bride and groom," she demands, and Nicki and Josh move to her side. "Nicole, you and your father will walk down the aisle. You can stand over there until we're ready for you. The bridal party?" she asks, and then she arranges us in order.

Jen is in front of me with another of Josh's football friends, and the rest of the bridal party is lined up in front of them.

Josh walks first up toward the place where an altar will be set up tomorrow.

The wedding isn't set up yet since hotel guests will be using the pool most of the day tomorrow, but I can imagine how gorgeous the whole effect will be with the shimmering water bouncing shadows off the buildings surrounding us.

Like something out of a bridal magazine, a platform will jut out over the pool, and that's where the bride, groom, and officiant will stand. The rest of us will stand on stairs, each one of us one level down from each other. After the ceremony, the platform will be transformed into the head table, which means the entire bridal party will sit over the water looking out over the tables filled with guests.

It's beautiful, but something tells me water and bridal gowns don't really mix. Or bridesmaids' gowns.

Stella cues the next couple when it's time to walk, and I feel like I have some things to say to Luke, but Jen is right in front of me and the last thing I want to do is fuel gossip at my brother's wedding.

So instead, I focus on the scenery. It's technically considered a rooftop wedding since it's on the top of the building where it's located, but it's the fourteenth level of the hotel, so towers stand tall all around us.

It's a perfect Vegas evening as the palm trees around the pool area sway with a gentle breeze. The heat of the day is setting with the sun, and the wedding will take place around this same time tomorrow night. It'll be perfect.

Each of the couples makes their way slowly down the aisle, and soon Jen and her escort head off.

That leaves Luke and me semi-alone.

"Your brother can't know," he murmurs to me as Jen and her guy slow their pace at Stella's command.

"Nobody can," I whisper-yell.

"Elbow out, Best Man, and Maid of Honor, arm through his. GO!" Stella yells even though she's not that far away from us. I wonder how much Josh and Nicki are paying this broad. Clearly they went for the cheaper package since she didn't even bother to learn our names.

Luke juts his elbow out, brushing my rib cage in the process. A dart of need pulses through me.

I shoot him a glare, and he holds in a laugh as I slide my arm through his.

I both love and hate being this close to him again.

I want him.

God, do I want him.

"No, I mean he *really* can't find out. He warned us all off when he invited you to move out here, and he specifically said he trusts me to take care of you the same way he would." He's whisper-yelling, too.

I glance over at him, and his eyes are focused forward. "You're supposed to be like an older brother to me?"

He glances at me, too, and there's a certain heat that passes between us. He's about to respond when Stella screeches at us. "Eyes forward!"

I turn toward the altar to appease her. This must be the longest damn aisle in the history of aisles.

He exhales. "Ellie, last night was…" he trails off, and I wish he wasn't whispering so I could hear his tone. "Hot," he finishes. "But it can't go beyond last night. You're my best friend's little sister, so that makes you off-limits."

Off-limits?

He just made it even hotter. Now it's forbidden. Now I definitely want it again.

I sigh. "I suppose it was him you were bragging to this morning?"

"Who else would it have been?" he asks wearily. "And I wasn't bragging."

"Like hell you weren't!" I exclaim the best I can in a whisper.

"Less talking!" Stella yells at us, and then we're nearing the altar and we're forced to let go of each other to move our separate ways.

But that conversation sure doesn't feel like it's over.

"What's going on with you two?" Jen whispers to me once I take my place next to her.

"With who?" I whisper back, playing dumb.

She rolls her eyes. "Isn't that the guy from the club you were dancing with?"

Oh shit.

In my little plan to keep this a secret, I totally forgot that Jen was there, too, and that she may have been lucid enough to remember the hot guy we met by the bar.

I blow out a breath. "I don't want anything to distract from Nicki's weekend," I say.

Her eyes get super round and her jaw falls open. "So something *did* happen."

"Ladies, quiet!" Stella yells at us, and Nicki shoots me a look like *come on, dude, just help me get through this.*

"We'll talk later," I say, hoping it's enough to brush her grilling off forever but knowing it definitely isn't.

When we're done with the actual rehearsal for tomorrow, we're ushered toward a restaurant where a whole section is dedicated to our little party.

And, of course, just like tomorrow night, Nicki and Josh sit in the middle of the table, and the rest of the bridal party sits in order on either side of them. That means the bride and groom separate Luke and me when I feel like I have a lot more to say to him, and Jen is on my right currently waiting for me to tell her what happened last night.

"You can't tell anyone," I say softly once I see Nicki and Josh talking to Stella. Jen's eyes go round again.

"Okay, but before you say anything at all, isn't this so exciting and totally cliché? The maid of honor and the best man are, like, *supposed* to hook up, aren't they? Isn't it some unwritten rule?"

I stare at her like she's stupid. "No! What if the maid of honor is married?"

"Then she'd be the *matron* of honor, and no such rule exists to my knowledge."

I roll my eyes. "Okay, fine. What if the best man is married?"

She thinks for a minute. "Affair." She cracks up like it's the funniest joke ever, but cheating isn't really all that funny to me.

"We did the one-night thing. I had no idea he was Josh's best man. And neither of us wants anyone to know, so keep your trap shut."

She looks offended as her hand flies to her chest. "I won't tell anybody!"

"Tell anybody what?" Nicki asks, looking at the two of us.

I'm positive I look guilty, and Jen has never been much of a liar.

"About your present!" Jen says almost gleefully, and thank the Lord, Nicki buys it.

"Oooh, what is it? Tell me, tell me, tell me!" Nicki says, her eyes lighting up.

Jen shakes her head then mock zips her lips and pretends to throw away the key, and man I wish I could find that key and hide it so she can't unzip.

Nicki's attention is called away again, and I glare at Jen. "Keep them zipped."

She holds up two fingers as if to say *Scout's Honor*, and then dinner is served and we focus on that.

My dad gives a surprisingly emotional speech about Josh and how he always imagined what kind of girl he'd marry, and then Nicki's dad gives a similar speech for his daughter.

And then it's Luke's turn.

"I'm Luke, the best man and also the better receiver," he begins, drawing a big laugh from the small crowd. "I couldn't be happier for my best friend and the woman who will become his wife tomorrow. Josh and I have only been playing together a year, but he's like a much younger brother to me."

Another laugh.

Great, this guy's not just ridiculously hot and fantastic in bed. He's also charming and hilarious.

"As someone who once sat in the same seat where Josh is sitting now, I have a word of advice."

Wait a minute.

He sat in Josh's chair?

Like, literally?

Or is he saying he's been in the chair as the groom at a rehearsal dinner?

Has Luke been *married* before?

Man, when I go in on a one-night stand, I really go all in. I know literally nothing about this guy.

I didn't even know he played football professionally, though I could see why he'd leave out that particular detail to someone who didn't immediately recognize him. Maybe that's one of the things he liked about me.

"I saved the good stuff for tomorrow's speech, but I'll end tonight with this: Never go to bed angry. Stay up and fight," he says, drawing roaring applause from the room.

The maid of honor is not expected to give a speech, for which I'm grateful since I don't really want to follow funny Hot Luke with something lame of my own.

Josh talks next, and he thanks everyone for coming and gets emotional as he looks at Nicki and talks about the life they're going to share.

And that's it. The night's still young, but the rehearsal is about over.

People mingle and drink, and Nicki is briefing the bridesmaids on the plan for tomorrow while I try to keep my eyes on her rather than edging over toward Luke. Nicki is called away by Stella, and I let my eyes feast for a beat.

He looks over at me, and our eyes lock for a second when I look away.

I blow out a breath, and then I head back to my seat to grab my phone where I left it on the table when I overhear Luke say to Josh, "Will Pepper be a problem for your sister?"

I glance up as I see Josh shaking his head. "She won't care."

I won't care about someone named Pepper?

Who the hell is Pepper? Isn't that a nickname for Penelope?

Is Luke seeing somebody? Does he *live* with somebody?

Is that the ex-wife? The current wife? The ex-girlfriend? A kid?

Did he sleep with me when he's involved with someone else?

I'm so confused.

These are the questions that roll through my mind in a split second, and I have no idea when I'll get the answers.

Not tonight, apparently, because Nicki's ready to finish her briefing, and by the time we're done chatting, all the men have cleared out except for Josh, who's waiting to bid his fiancée goodnight.

But Hot Luke is gone, and the next time I'll see him is tomorrow when he's wearing a tux and I'm torn halfway between lust and animosity.

CHAPTER 10

As I go to bed alone, I can't stop thinking about Luke. If I close my eyes and concentrate, I can still smell him in this room. I can still feel his tongue on my body.

I blow out a breath and force my eyes open. That's not helping.

I do an Instagram search for him and come up blank after sorting through fifty or so accounts with the same name. There are a few photos tagged with a hashtag and his name, but there's no user by the name of Luke Dalton that matches Hot Luke. Though there is one who appears to be obsessed with fish and another who looks like he's about ten years old.

He's not on Twitter, either, or Facebook.

I stop my search there.

So he's not a social media guy. Not everybody is, though I'd think if he wanted the status as a fan favorite, he'd need to let people into his life a little more.

Maybe he doesn't want that status, but based on his looks alone, he probably *is* a favorite of the ladies.

And I had sex with him.

I glance over at the windows.

Right there up against those windows.

I let out a soft sigh as it all comes back to me. It was just last night, but somehow it feels like ages ago.

I'm nervous for tomorrow. I don't like keeping secrets from my brother or from Nicki, but neither Luke nor I want them to find out, especially not this weekend when they deserve the focus.

And so I'll pretend.

I'll pretend like I didn't have sex with Hot Luke.

I'll pretend like I don't want to do it again.

I'll put on a little act.

It shouldn't be that hard. Right?

It's another fitful night's sleep. I can't stop thinking about Luke, or the fact that I'm supposed to *move in with him* for a while until I can find a job and a place to live. My brother would surely help me out financially on those fronts, but he's a little busy, you know, *getting married*, and then he'll be on his honeymoon. His top priority at the moment certainly isn't helping his little sister find living arrangements.

I can't even stay at Josh and Nicki's because of their renovations, but even if they weren't having work done, it would be weird at this point to back out of this arrangement to live with Luke. My brother would want a reason why I suddenly had a change of heart, and I'd have to admit why I did, and then I'd be doing the one thing Luke requested in keeping what happened between the two of us.

So I'm stuck.

All the girls are meeting up in Nicki's room for breakfast followed by a day of getting ready, so after my shower, I head in that direction. Nadine throws open the door. "Happy Nicki's wedding day," she says with a smile.

I laugh. "Same to you." I beeline for the bride, who's holding a mimosa and standing by the window while she talks on the phone.

I lace my arms around her from behind and give her a hug.

"No, I said *gardenias*. That doesn't sound anything like *stargazers*! They smell awful!" She's yelling at the poor florist.

"Just fix it!" She ends the call and tosses her phone onto a nearby table before taking a long sip of her mimosa.

"Happy wedding day!" I squeal, and she takes a deep breath.

"Thanks," she murmurs.

"I'm here to handle those calls from here on out, my friend. You just focus on marrying my brother."

Her eyes dart to me, and she looks a little...guilty?

"What's wrong?" I ask.

"I'm just so nervous." Her voice is a whisper.

Okay, well, I'm probably not the best candidate to listen to her say all the reasons why she's nervous to marry *my brother*, but I'm also her best friend, so I tough it out. "About what?"

"He's, like, the last guy I'll ever have sex with," she says, and she's starting to wail a little. "And what if I hate being a football wife? It's always going to be about him and his career, not about me and mine."

I feel awkward for a beat as I really have no idea what to say. I don't know what being a *football wife* entails, and I've honestly never really thought about it apart from what the ladies at the bachelorette party mentioned. I know what it's like being a *football sister*, and most of the time it's not a big deal. Nolan is a common enough last name that people don't stop me and ask about my brother.

But she's my girl, and I try to come up with some words of support.

Someone else beats me to the punch, though. It feels weird not being the one who is there for her in this moment after I've been there for her every step of the way since we were sophomores in high school and became fast friends at volleyball camp.

"Honey, it's true," Nadine says, sidling up next to her and wrapping an arm around her shoulder. "But football careers are short. Retirement is long. It may be about him and his career for the next few years, but then you have the rest of forever together to do whatever you want."

"Is that what you're banking on?" Nicki asks, and Nadine nods.

"You've known him since before his football career took off, right?" Nadine asks.

"Yeah," Nicki says.

"So you know the real *him*. The guy inside. He'll be that guy regardless of what he's doing for a career. Besides, having doubts on your wedding day is natural. It's like a rite of passage."

Nicki nods and sniffles. "You're right." She draws in a deep breath. "Okay, thanks. I'm good now."

"Every bride deserves at least one meltdown on her wedding day." Nadine winks.

We're in the middle of getting ready when my phone buzzes with a new text. We've had finger sandwiches and laughed a lot as the mini-meltdown has been put to rest. My make-up is perfection, my hair is getting the royal treatment from someone named Daisy, and showtime begins in under ninety minutes with pictures in less than an hour.

I pick up my phone to check it in case it's something wedding-related. I don't recognize the number.

Unknown: *I need to talk to you.*

Me: *Who is this?*

Unknown: *The best man. It's about the wedding. Best man and maid of honor shit.*

Me: *How did you get my number?*

Luke: *Your brother gave it to me.*

Okay, well that makes sense and I don't even know why it matters.

Me: *I'm in the middle of getting my hair done but I can meet you in twenty minutes or so when I go to my room to change into my dress.*

Luke: *Same room as the other night?*
I blush. Hard.
Me: *Same room.*
Luke: *See you then.*

Daisy finishes curling my hair, and then she does some wavy thing to it and pins only part of it back so my dark blonde locks flow freely down my back.

"I'm going to go put my dress on," I say to Nicki, and she grunts some response as her make-up artist works on her eyes.

I rush down to my room, slip into the pale pink dress that makes my skin look a golden tan, and check myself in the mirror. The warm tones they used make my blue eyes pop, and I might just have to order the colors and brands they used because *damn* I look good.

A knock at my door pulls me away from the mirror, and my heart beats double time.

He's here.

When I open the door, my knees nearly buckle beneath me.

Luke stands there in a tuxedo. My eyes travel from his feet in his dress shoes, up his powerful legs to the hips that were slamming against my backside, to his abdomen that has those fine cuts of muscle, to his broad chest and shoulders made stronger from his athletic background, to his handsome face with eyes that heat as they meet mine.

"Holy fuck, Ellie. You're...that dress..." His eyes dip to my cleavage and back to my face. "And your hair..."

My lips tip up in a smile. He's flustered, and the fact that I'm the one who's making him that way makes me feel the same way. "Right back at you, Hot Luke."

He grins, and my knees actually do buckle a little.

An ache throbs between my legs.

The bed is *right there*. And the windows...we could just do it against the windows and then he won't mess up my hair.

I lean on the doorframe for support. "We, uh, have like five minutes if you want to..."

He chuckles, and then he sighs as he averts his gaze from mine. "As much as I'd love to, I already told you, I can't take advantage of my best friend's little sister."

"It's not *taking advantage* when I'm the one offering," I say, a little exasperated as the sting of rejection bites at me. "Besides, my brother is marrying *my* best friend. Why does he care if one of his friends hooks up with his sister?"

Luke laughs. "Trust me, Sexy Ellie, I want to. But this is bro code. I work with your brother, and I'm not the right guy for you anyway. Besides, I thought you were still mad at me for bragging about our night."

I sigh and cross my arms over my chest. I know it's both making me look angry and pushing my breasts together, which is exactly what I want. "That's right. I *am* mad."

I earn the intended effect as his eyes flick down to my chest again. He laughs. "I'm not convinced. You just tried to seduce me."

"Whatever. So why are you here, then? What did you need to talk about?"

"Uh," he says a little dumbly, and I try not to laugh. "Oh, right. Your brother is having this whole thing. He isn't sure he wants to get married."

"What?" I screech. I just sat through calming the bride down as Nadine convinced her she does want this. Now the groom, too? Maybe they *shouldn't* get married if they're both having doubts.

"Something about how he'll only get to bang her for the rest of his life. And I think it might sort of be my fault," he admits.

I open my door wider and motion for him to follow me. I stop near the foot of the bed, and he stops a few paces away.

Good Lord this man is a real treat to look at, and he smells divine, too. Some sort of cologne he definitely wasn't wearing when we hooked up.

Did he wear it for me?

I somehow doubt it, but a little part of me hopes he did.

"So why is this your fault, and why are you telling me?" I ask.

"Those are two complicated questions, so I'll start with the easier one. You're her best friend and his sister. You know both of them probably better than anyone. Do you think they should get married?"

I nod. "They belong together. Nicki just went through a whole thing this morning, too. I think it's natural to have doubts." I repeat what Nadine said.

"It is," he says. He clears his throat. "I, uh, did when I got married. But the difference is that I should have listened to mine."

God, I'd love to dig more into that...

But the wedding is in an hour. We need to get my brother's head on straight and get them down the aisle.

And if Luke is about to become my roommate, I'll have time to learn more about him.

Even though now I'm dying to know if the ex he just broke up with is this wife he's talking about.

"He keeps harping on the fact that I had a one-night stand and he won't get to have those anymore. Do you know how fucking hard it is to hear him talk about *my* one-night stand knowing it was with his *sister*?"

"Uh...sorry?" I say, not exactly sure what he wants me to say to that.

"It's not your fault," he mutters. "Sorry. It's been a long day already. Can you help me? Tell me what to say to him to convince him he wants this, because I'm not entirely convinced people *should* get married."

"You don't want to get married again?" I ask, surprised.

"Focus, Ellie," he says with a touch of frustration, and somehow he's even sexier when he's just a little frustrated. It might even be sort of fun to poke at him. "That's not the issue at hand."

He's right.

"Okay. Take me to my brother and we'll get this straightened out."

He nods once, and I put on my shoes and grab my clutch. I slip my phone, room key, and lipstick in, and then we head toward the groom's suite so I can do some damage control.

CHAPTER 11

"She's waiting to walk down that aisle toward the man she loves more than anything in the world. Are you going to be there?" I ask my brother.

He looks up at me, and I can see the uncertainty in his eyes.

"You can't do this to her," I whisper. "She loves you, you big idiot. I know it's scary, but everyone is scared on their wedding day."

"Yeah, I know. Ask Luke," he says, and I narrow my eyes at Luke for a beat because what the hell did he say that might've put these doubts in my brother's head, and for the love of God, why would Josh choose him as his best man?

"Luke and I talked. We both know how right you two are for each other. Luke and his ex just...weren't. They didn't have that same spark you and Nicki do." I'm talking out of my ass, but it seems to be working. "She's your soul mate, Josh. You know that. She's had a crush on you since we were in high school, and she's been there for you since the two of you first got together. You know she loves you for who you are, not because you play football or because you have money in the bank."

He nods. "Yeah." He scrubs a hand along his jaw as he thinks it through. "I love her. So much that it scares me sometimes."

"I know," I say, and I squeeze his hand. I glance up at Luke, and our eyes catch. My chest aches. I want what Nicki and Josh have—maybe minus the wedding day jitter doubts. Part of me thought I could've had it with Todd, but that didn't pan out. "And that's why I know you're both ready for this."

He nods. "Thanks, Ellie Belly."

My cheeks burn at his term of endearment as I pray Luke somehow missed it and won't call me that forever now.

Josh blows out a breath. "Okay." He squeezes my forearm. "Let's do this thing."

"You better get moving, Osh Kosh ba-Josh," I say, glancing at the clock. "You're not even wearing shoes, and you've got pictures by the pool before the ladies get out there. You know you're not allowed to see Nicki until she walks down the aisle."

"I've got it from here," Luke says.

"See you out there," I say to my brother, and Luke walks me to the door.

"Thanks for your help," he says, and the sweet feeling of victory—of overcoming a little obstacle with him that pulled us a little closer together—rushes through my chest.

"No problem," I say softly. And then I punch him in the arm. He grabs the spot and makes a face like it really hurt even though I know it didn't. "But next time, let me know it's a freaking emergency before I blow you off for a half hour while I get my hair done."

He laughs. "Next time? You really think this might happen again?"

I giggle, too, and then I shrug. "Maybe not *this exact situation*, but you know what I mean."

His eyes twinkle, and then he opens the door. "See you out there, Ellie Belly," he says. I shoot him a glare, but it fades as his eyes linger on me for a beat. My stomach flips, and then I seem to snap out of it as I realize I need to get moving. But, *damn*, do I want his eyes to linger like that again.

Like they did Thursday night.

I don't have time to dwell on it, though.

I run back to the bridal suite.

"Where the hell have you been?" Nicki demands when I walk in.

"I went to talk to Josh after I got dressed," I admit, without actually admitting the reason why. I take a beat to study my best friend. She's the perfect portrait of a glowing, beautiful bride. "You look gorgeous."

She ignores my compliment as her eyes widen. "Why'd you go talk to him? Is everything okay?"

I nod and smile. "Everything's fine. Just wanted to see my big brother," I lie. Neither of them ever has to know the other freaked out. It's part of the maid of honor and best man's duties to ensure a smooth day, and making sure the groom is waiting there at the end of the aisle when the bride walks down it seems to fall under that umbrella.

Pictures are taken and smiles abound, and before I know it, the bridesmaids are lining up to make our way down the aisle. When Luke steps into place beside me, that cologne pulls at my senses and nerves flitter through my chest.

"You still look beautiful," he murmurs, and my cheeks redden at his words as my chest tightens.

It isn't fair.

I don't want him to tell me things like that when he's vowed not to act on this steamy attraction between us. And he's right. I'm still mad at him for bragging about us. *To my brother.*

I slide my arm through his elbow. We probably have some time before I *really* need to do that, but I like being close to him, and he smells good, and he isn't exactly pushing me away. "You still look like Hot Luke," I whisper back, and he keeps his eyes forward but his lips tip up with a smile.

Stella directs Nadine and her husband, Richard, to make their way down the aisle. She signals the next bridesmaid and groomsman, and soon enough, it's our turn.

I feel like there's so much I want to say to Luke, but I don't dare say a word as all eyes assembled in the crowd seem to turn toward the two of us.

Do we look good walking down the aisle together?

Well, duh. It's *Luke*. He'd look good escorting a clown down the aisle.

Could this be us someday, with him already waiting at the end of the aisle like Josh is as I wait to walk down with my dad?

Doubtful, but damn, a girl can dream.

Our eyes meet more than once as we each watch our best friends marry, and I wish I could decode what he's thinking.

I still know next to nothing about him...except now I know that he was married before.

Hot Luke is kind of a mystery, and that sort of makes him...dare I say...even hotter?

Once the ceremony is over, the bridal party meets in a conference room for a quick celebration and toast to the newly married couple while the guests are ushered to another area outside for a cocktail hour. I help Nicki in the bathroom, by far the worst part of my duties as MOH and a feat that's sort of comparable to peeling an onion to get the juice in the middle without messing up any of the layers. I lose track of Luke until we head back outside, where the aisle, altar, and guest chairs have been transformed into a banquet area.

A long table for the wedding party sits on the platform over the pool, lights twinkling in the near twilight as the sun begins to set behind the tall buildings circling us. It's romantic and gorgeous, somehow merging a *spare no expense* feel with a casual, intimate vibe. The whole thing just perfectly sets the scene for the reception of these two lovebirds.

We line up and the deejay who's serving as emcee calls Nadine and Richard first to make their way toward their seats. They walk up, and he twirls her, and it's all very cute. I watch as the other couples go, all doing equally cute things even though some of them only met last night, and my heart picks up speed as nerves set in.

I'm about to be introduced, and I have to walk out on Luke's arm, and we don't have anything cute planned like everyone else had.

"What should we do?" I whisper-yell.

Luke glances over at me with his brows dipped. "What do you mean?"

"The maid of honor, Ellie Nolan, with the best man, Luke Dalton!"

"Spin me," I whisper yell as we walk to the center of the reception area. He doesn't quite get my meaning, and he spins us both, and I grab onto his hand and twist myself around.

And, because this is *my* life, my heel gets caught in a crack along the cement walkway. The heel doesn't break completely, but it's not quite glued to my shoe the same way it was before.

Great.

Just what I need.

A broken shoe at the start of the reception as I trip in front of the hottest guy I've ever seen in my life and, of course, the entire group gathered to celebrate my brother's wedding.

Luke catches me at the last second, and it *almost* looks like I didn't totally take a spill as I wind up tight in his arms. I cling to his shoulders, and our eyes meet—his worried as I nearly topple to the ground, and mine probably rabid like a damn wild animal as I look upon the object of my lust who just saved me from a really embarrassing fall.

Now I'm in his arms and I want to kiss him but every-freaking-body in the room is watching us.

I'm shaky, somewhat from the almost-fall but more from being so close to Luke. He straightens me. "You okay?" he murmurs as I suck in a deep breath, still clinging to him and really just getting a mouthful of his cologne.

It sounds grosser than it is. It's fucking magic.

I want to lick his neck.

"Fine," I gasp, and then we're supposed to part so we can each walk up the stairs toward our seats on the platform over the pool.

Thankfully there's a railing behind our chairs, because I sure as hell would fall right into the water with the way my knees are trembling.

I glance over and find Luke smiling at me as we each take our place, and *God* that smile just gets me every time. I can't tell if he's smiling at me or laughing at me. I tell myself it's a reassuring, friendly smile. If I tell myself he's laughing at me, well, I'm not sure my fragile ego could actually take that.

My knees bang together as I think of his smile. I grip the back of the chair in front of me as I stand, and then the bride and groom are announced so eyes aren't on the two of us anymore. Thank God.

I exhale a long breath and try to regain my composure, but literally falling into Luke's arms sure threw me off balance. I keep my eyes on Nicki and Josh even though I want to look over. I feel like he's looking at me. The side of my face burns with his gaze, but when I glance over, he's looking at the happy couple dancing their way across the floor just as he should be.

He said I'm off-limits to him...but he's not off-limits to me.

He's about to become my new roommate. I'm going to have to just get past the bragging thing, though it still sort of makes him out to be an asshole. But he's not. He seems like a good guy, barring that one indiscretion of bragging about a one-night stand in the middle of a Starbucks.

Which was even dumber on his part considering he's a professional football player and anyone could've overheard. He's lucky it was just me.

We already know we're fire beneath the sheets...though I still want to know why he jetted out afterward.

And maybe, just maybe, I'll have a drink or two tonight and get up the nerve to actually ask him.

CHAPTER 12

He holds me as we sway to the romantic song, and I'm about a millisecond from resting my head on his shoulder, but I force myself not to.

Dancing with him just feels so...right.

Except when my heel keeps catching on the dance floor. It still hasn't broken off completely, but it's not doing well. I'm doing my best to ignore it.

I'm clouded by the wine I've had, which is just about the perfect place to be, and I *want* him again. So badly I can taste it. Or him.

Our bodies move in tandem, sort of like they did when he had me shoved up against a window (except not naked and not from behind), and the whole setting is a backdrop for the start of something really romantic.

I draw in a deep breath, and then I move back and look him in the eye. His are heated, but maybe that's just how they always look and I'm imagining things. Or it's possible the wine is clouding my judgment. "Can I ask you something?" I say softly.

One of his brows dips and it's freaking adorable. "Sure." His tone is hesitant.

"Why'd you run out on me after we had such a nice time?"

"On Thursday?" he asks.

I nod.

"I needed to get home to take care of some things."

Well that's sure as hell a non-answer if I've ever heard one.

"How long ago did you and your ex end things?" I ask next. He said a couple months, and even though he said he's over her, he might just need more time. And if he needs time, it's probably out of the question to even entertain the idea of being with him...not that he's given me any indication at all that he's on board with that idea.

He looks down at me, his face blank. "You're full of questions."

"I guess I just...I don't know." I blink, and then I confess, "I'd like to get to know the guy I'm about to be living with."

"Your brother kind of made it sound like we'd each stick to our own sides of my house." His eyes are on mine, and maybe I don't know him at all, but I can still see a little twinkle there. He's teasing me even though his words indicate otherwise. He seems like he's hard to read, but I think I'm starting to figure him out.

"Is that what you want?" I ask, my voice low as I'm not really sure how he'll answer.

He hitches up a shoulder, and maybe I'm not figuring him out at all. Then he sighs. "My divorce was official a little over four years ago. My most recent ex and I ended things a few months ago."

Aha! So an ex-wife *and* an ex-girlfriend. That answers that question. "Well, you already know about my most recent ex."

He chuckles. "Yeah, you mentioned him."

"I was twenty-one when your divorce was official. Possibly twenty."

He chuckles. "You're young. You never mentioned your age before."

"How old are you?"

"Thirty-one. Fucking ancient for a football player."

I raise a brow, and then there goes my filter because why the hell would I want to point these things out to him when I'm trying to convince him we belong together? That's right. Because of wine. "You're six years older than me. That means when you started high school, I was around eight. When you started college, I was probably twelve."

"And when I was drafted into the league, you were learning how to drive a car," he finishes.

"It's not *that* big a difference. Not now, anyway. I feel like once you start your career and become an adult, ages don't really matter."

"That's when life experience starts to matter instead. I've been in the league nine years. I've been married and divorced. I've had multiple relationships that have shown me what I want out of life. What do *you* want out of life?"

Would it be inappropriate to say *you* here? Probably so. I'm showing my age and my sheltered life. I barely know this guy and the hopeless romantic in me is already head over heels. I need to put a pin in that. I open my mouth to answer when the song changes and the bridal party dance is over. Josh slings an arm around Luke's neck, forcing me out of his arms.

I don't know if I'll get the chance to be back in them.

"The groomsmen are heading outside," Josh says, and I roll my eyes. It's his secret code for letting Luke know it's time to go to the other side of the pool area to smoke cigars, which is about the grossest thing in the world.

I wrinkle my nose in disgust, and to my surprise, Luke does, too.

"We already *are* outside, dude," he says.

Josh laughs. "I knew you'd say that, but come anyway. You don't have to smoke."

He heaves out a breath. "Fine. But when I'm coughing at workouts Monday morning, I'm telling coach it's your fault."

"Coach isn't expecting us on Monday," Josh says.

"I'll still be there."

"Of course you will," my brother mutters, and it's another tiny insight into Luke's personality.

He's the kind of guy who will show up no matter what. He cares about his body—both what he puts into it and taking care of it. That's probably why it's utter perfection.

He heads off with my brother, and I take it as my cue to head back to my chair to sit for a few minutes. As I walk up the steps toward my seat, though, I forget about my semi-broken heel.

I stumble on a step and completely lose my balance. Instead of falling backward into the railing, though, I fall forward.

And falling forward off the steps means I don't just trip and fall onto the stairs. No, of course not. That would be too easy. That would be too *dry*.

Instead, I fall right into the damn swimming pool.

I hear the gasps from dry land only when my submerged head finds the surface.

I wipe the water out of my eyes, smearing my make-up beyond recognition. One of the fake lashes I was wearing is on my fingertips when I pull my hand away. I feel the other one sticking right to my cheek, and I peel it off.

Someone else yells, and a few people start laughing, and then a crowd gathers to watch the clumsy, very wet maid of honor as she frantically and futilely tries to make her way toward the stairs to get out of the pool.

It's not like it's deep. I'm only in three or four feet of water, and I can stand.

But what I didn't think I even needed to account for was how freaking heavy the layers of tulle and silk would become when submerged in water.

I'm still wearing my heels, and one is definitely broken now, as I try to walk across the pool, but it's like I'm stuck in quicksand. People are watching, but no one seems to know what the hell to do to help the idiot in the water without getting wet themselves.

And then I'm engulfed by a wave as someone else splashes into the water.

When I wipe the water and the surprise away from my eyes, I spot who it is.

And when he comes up out of the water—still in his tux, though he removed the jacket to jump into the pool to save me—our eyes meet. Mine must surely be racoon eyes with makeup bleeding in every direction, but he looks worried. Well, and he also looks like a goddamn fairy tale merman as he emerges from the water, the water glistening on his glowing skin like droplets that want to cling on for dear life because once they drop off, they don't get to be close to him anymore.

I know the feeling.

He reaches for me and hooks an arm around my waist, and then he helps me walk over to the steps. He gathers the weighty part of the dress in his arms, and then he squeezes it to get some of the moisture out with each step I take up and out of the water.

I feel this weird mix of completely awful that I ruined my brother's reception and totally elated that Hot Luke was the one who jumped in to save me.

I'm leaning more toward elated, though.

Because the moment I met Hot Luke, I'm pretty sure my fairy tale began.

I can't wait to see where it leads next.

CHAPTER 13

The guests all clap when we're both out of the pool, and some attendants who work for the hotel bring us towels to dry off.

"Are you okay?" Nicki asks as I wrap a towel around my wet hair and use another one to rub away some of the bleeding makeup under my eyes. I look at the towel where I did my work. It's black.

I must look like a freaking disaster right now.

"Yeah, I'm okay," I mutter. "I'm so sorry."

I glance over at Luke. He does *not* look like a freaking disaster.

In fact, he looks somehow even more gorgeous. Water drips from his dark hair, which is semi-slicked back but too short to hold the slick so it just sticks up in perfect disarray, and his white shirt clings to his stomach, showcasing his washboard abs for everyone lucky enough to catch a glimpse.

My one-night stand.

My brother's best friend.

My hero.

My new roommate.

I sigh softly.

"What the hell happened?" Nicki asks. "Did someone push you?"

"No, no, nothing like that," I say. "I tripped. My heel was a little wobbly and I fell while I was walking up the stairs."

"Only you, Ellie, I swear," Josh says as he laughs, and it's total déjà vu as I'm transported to the last time he said those exact same words to me less than a week ago when Todd dumped me and I was fired in the same day. To be fair, it's a phrase he uses quite a bit around me.

"The bride and groom will now be cutting the cake," the deejay announces, and thankfully that takes the eyes off Luke and me.

I don't want to miss them cutting the cake or any of the other traditions at a wedding, but I'm soaked and this dress isn't getting any lighter and I'm fucking mortified. "I'm going to go dry off and change," I tell Nicki, and I start heading in toward the hotel.

"Wait up," Luke says from right behind me. "I'll go, too." He grabs his shoes, which he took off to dive in to save me, and we walk together toward the building.

"You okay?" he asks softly.

"Yes, I'm fine," I say. "Just embarrassed. Thanks for helping me."

He laughs. "Someone had to. You were flailing around in there, spinning in circles like you didn't know which way was out."

"Yeah, well, could've been anyone, and it had to be you," I mutter. The automatic doors open and we step through and head toward the elevator.

"What's that supposed to mean?" He presses the button for the elevator.

I blink, and I debate how much to say, and then I realize...screw it. I'm starting over in a new city. I have no job, no place of my own, no friends out here. I have nothing to lose by being perfectly honest except for some awkwardness with my new roommate, but you know what? Awkwardness never killed anybody. Did it?

I shake my head. He glances down at me with furrowed brows, and hell if it isn't the cutest thing I've ever seen. "I like you, Luke. And you keep doing things and saying things to make me like you more. But you already told me I'm forbidden fruit, and I'm trying so damn hard to act like you're not the Prince Charming of the ultimate fairy tale, but you just keep proving that you are."

I'm babbling, and I realize that.

He pulls me into his arms. "It's okay," he soothes, rubbing circles on my back.

My face is pressed to his chest. His hard, firm chest. "See?" I say, my face smashed against his wet shirt, muffling my voice. "Even this is Prince Charming material."

"Oh, sweet, Sexy Ellie," he says softly. He presses a soft kiss to the top of my head. "I promise you, I'm no prince."

The elevator doors open, breaking up our intimate moment, and we pull apart to step on. It's a fairly full car, and we draw curious glances from the others as two wet people dressed up in their finest hop on board.

"Can you believe *I* fell in the pool and *she* jumped in to save me?" he says to the quiet car full of strangers, and awkward laughter erupts.

I smack him in the shoulder, laughing at him. The doors open and he gets off on the forty-third floor. "I'll come get you when I'm done," he says before the doors close, and I ride up to floor forty-seven as I wonder how long I'll be waiting for him—or if he'll move quickly and be waiting on me.

When I get to the mirror, I find that the damage is even worse than I imagined.

I scrub my face clean. I can start over on my make-up once I get this damn heavy dress off.

I take a quick body shower to get the chlorine off, not daring to mess with the rat nest that's my hair. I'll need a little time to get the pins out of the wet mess.

I'm just toweling dry when there's a knock at the door. I think we can all guess who it is.

Of course I'm in my towel and not dressed yet when he shows up. Why would it be any other way?

But you know what? I want him, and I want him to want me back.

And seeing a girl that he had sex with clad only in a teeny-tiny hotel towel has to be at least a *little* tempting, right?

I see the fluffy hotel robe on my way by the closet to answer the door, and I take all of a millisecond to ignore that it's even there. A flimsy towel that barely covers the goodie bits versus a huge fluffy robe? If I'm going for temptation, the flimsy towel wins.

I throw open the door, and it's not Luke at all.

Guess those little peephole thingies come in handy.

It's.

My.

Dad.

"Oh, gosh, Ellie!" He shields his eyes. "I'm sorry!"

"No, Dad, don't be," I mutter. "I'm the one who's sorry." My face burns as I realize I nearly flashed my own father all the goods, and *that* is when Hot Luke decides to show up at my door.

Dry as a bone.

Hair restyled perfectly.

Wearing a suit that's not a tux but that still makes him look hella delish.

And once again, catching me in a completely and totally embarrassing situation.

"Were you expecting someone else?" my dad asks, completely oblivious to the fact that Luke is standing directly behind him.

"No!" I exclaim, trying to think fast. "I, uh, figured it was Nicki or one of the other bridesmaids checking up on me."

"Well it's me checking up on you," he says.

"I came to check on you, too," Luke says smoothly, finally alerting my dad to the fact that he's standing there.

"I'm fine. But please, everyone, come on in." I open the door, and both my dad and Luke walk in. My cheeks burn as Luke's eyes move straight to the window where he had me bent over as he banged into me from behind.

He glances at me and raises a brow, and I want to just curl into a ball and die right about now.

I rummage through my suitcase and I find dry underwear. I turn to the closet for the black dress I packed as a just in case, and then I lock myself in the bathroom.

So much for seducing Luke.

I put on a light smattering of make-up, unpin my hair as quickly as I can, spray about a gallon of detangler on it, and try to comb it out. Ultimately I twist it into a bun and call it good. The pictures have already been taken, so it's not like I'll be ruining those with this fresh new look straight from the depths of hell.

I pair my dress with black flats because hell if I'm getting back into heels, and then I turn to my dad and Luke, who seem to be shooting the shit, and I say, "Ready?"

This is not exactly how I planned for the last ten minutes to go, but it is what it is.

The elevator ride down to the reception is not quite as exciting as the ride up, and when we emerge back into the pool area, everyone has basically forgotten the poor girl who fell into the pool and the hot football megastar who saved her.

But I didn't forget.

He may have told me he's no prince, but I beg to differ. Or, at the very least, I want to find out for myself.

CHAPTER 14

Luke runs off to be with the guys, and there aren't any more organized dances where I get the shot to be close to him, so instead I hang with Jen. She's also here without a date, so we're just two single bridesmaids chatting about when in the hell it'll be our turn to wear the white dress.

We eat cake and we drink wine and we fight over the bouquet when Nicki tosses it. I'm not the one who catches it, for the record. Delia is.

So at least one fairy tale cliché skips past me.

By the time I slide into my bed (all alone, as planned from the start even though I had hope things would turn out differently), I'm freaking exhausted.

I wonder where Luke is. I wonder if he's still awake.

I wonder if he's thinking about me the way I'm thinking about him.

I force the thought away. But he did save me today, and it felt like more than friendship.

I shoot off a text since I have his number now.

Me: *Thanks for saving me today.*

His reply comes a few minutes later.

Luke: *Happy to help.*

I try to decode some hidden meaning in those three words, but I'm pretty sure there isn't any. He's just a nice guy who was helping out the clumsy girl who fell in the water.

I'm not sure why that makes me a little sad.

In the morning, my first thought when I wake is of Luke. I think I even dreamed of him.

I wake up with a new tenacity. He told me no—multiple times—and maybe it's time I actually listen. I do, after all, still have to live with him, and it would probably be in my best interest to respect his wishes even though I'm still sure we belong together.

I can't be the only one who feels it.

That one night we shared was more than a spark. It was a freaking volcano.

What I'm feeling now is the aftershocks, I think. Sparks here and there from the fiery lava that isn't even starting to cool.

I don't imagine I'll see him this morning since immediate family is supposed to gather for brunch. It's being held in a special suite where the staff brought all the presents last night so we can watch the happy couple open their gifts. I'll also be responsible for recording who got them what so they can churn out their thank you cards after the honeymoon.

When I get to the suite and knock on the door, want to venture a guess as to who opens it?

Not someone in my immediate family, that's for sure.

Thank God I opted for a shower this morning, though if I'd have known Hot Luke was going to be here, I might've put forth a little more effort.

"What are you doing here?" I ask.

"I'm supposed to help with the gifts," he says.

"I'm the sister." The words tumble out of my mouth, and it's about the dumbest thing I can think of to say, but it's also the *only* thing I can think of to say.

"Yeah, I sort of got that. And the bride's best friend. So you're basically doubly responsible for being here."

I laugh. "I don't know why I said that. I just...wasn't expecting to see you this morning, I guess."

He shoots me a tight, fake smile. "Well surprise!" He holds his hands out and waves them around before he opens the door wider to let me in, and I practically run past him. In one corner there's a table overflowing with gifts. This is going to take all damn day.

Nicki and Josh are giggling with their heads bent close together near the buffet table, and my mom and dad are talking to Nicki's parents. Nicki's little brother has his face in his phone on the couch, and the only other people here are Luke and me.

So even if I *wanted* to talk to someone aside from Luke Dalton, it looks like my only options are interrupting the newlyweds, walking into a conversation between parents, or sitting next to the seventeen-year-old kid who came along as a *surprise* eight years after Nicki was born.

I heave out a breath and opt for the simplest answer: the buffet table.

"Good morning," I say brightly, interrupting newlywed giggles which are probably sexual in nature given Nicki's rosy cheeks, but I don't ask, and I don't want to know.

"Hey," Josh says, his eyes never leaving his wife.

His *wife*. God, it's weird that Josh is freaking *married* now. He's a *husband*.

That's going to take some getting used to.

"Okay, I'll just sneak past you and grab some food," I say wholly to myself since they're still wrapped up in their own little world.

I fill my plate with eggs and fruit, and then I sit by myself at one of the little tables.

I glance up and see Luke approaching.

I can't seem to escape this guy. I'm also not sure I want to, but he's made it pretty clear he's not interested beyond the one night we shared.

"Looks like we're each other's best option for brunch entertainment," he says softly as he pulls out a chair beside me and slides into it.

I give him a wry smile. "Thanks for checking everyone else off the list first."

"To be fair, you definitely did the same thing but also eliminated me from your list when you came over here to sit by yourself with your lonely plate of food."

I narrow my eyes to a glare and stick a giant piece of watermelon in my mouth. I'm sure I look very attractive as I attempt to chomp it down to a normal sized piece of food.

His brows dip down. "Why the change of heart?"

I raise a brow. "You liked it better when I kept tripping over myself to get to you?"

He glances down at the table. "I wouldn't say that, exactly, but yesterday you were at least friendly toward me."

"I'm still friendly. I just realized that you don't like me the way I like you, so I need to put a pin in it." I help myself to another huge piece of watermelon.

"Yeah, I do like you the same way, Ellie," he says, and there's something really illicit about the way he says the words in a quiet, husky voice that's just for me. He glances around, and everyone else is still occupied in their own conversations. Over here, we just look like we're two people having a chat.

But it feels like a lot more as my heart races at his words.

My eyes meet his, and his burn at me with the same fire they did on our single night together.

"I'd go back on my word to your brother if I thought I was right for you," he says softly. "I think most of what he said was in jest, anyway. But that's the thing. I'm *not* right for you.

You're young, and you want the fairy tale happy ending with your Prince Charming. I'm a divorced, slightly older and definitely more cynical guy who thinks those make-believe stories are for children."

My chest feels hollow at his words. "Oh." The single word is all that comes out of my mouth, though my mind races.

"It'll be easier to live together if we're just friends," he says.

I nod. "Yeah. I know. Friends. And we still think this living together thing is a good idea?"

"I thought it was a terrible idea from the start, but I agreed anyway since it was for your brother," he says, gently pushing my shoulder the way an old pal would. "And I think if we back out now, they'll know something's up. So we're kind of stuck, don't you think?" He pauses as he lets me mull that over, and then he says, "I'm going to go grab some food."

I press my lips together and stare down at my plate while he gets up. I brush away that deflated feeling that pings through my chest.

He's cynical and he thinks fairy tales are make-believe stories for children?

Enter Ellie.

We may not end up together, but that doesn't mean I can't help him lighten up a tad in the meantime. He said it'll be easier to live together if we're friends, and I intend to become his actual friend...not just his best friend's little sister.

He returns with his plate of food that's mounded with more calories than I eat in a day and sits. "So, *friend*, which football team do you scream for on Sundays?"

I raise a brow. "The Aces?"

He chuckles and shovels in some eggs. "Right answer, but I doubt the sincerity when it sounds like a question."

"I'm not actually a football fan," I admit.

He looks at me in horror, like he didn't know such a creature actually existed.

What can I say? I'm a freaking unicorn.

I glance around to make sure everyone else is out of hearing distance. "Probably also the reason why I didn't know who you were the night we met."

"Ah, yes, it all makes sense now. Everyone knows Luke motherfuckin' Dalton."

I laugh. "What position do you play?"

"Wide receiver."

"So the same as Josh?" I ask.

He nods and raises a brow. "Impressive that you know that. Do you even watch the games?"

"I do," I say. "But, like, I have them *on*. I wouldn't say I *pay attention* to them. I guess I've just been around it my whole life. Josh has played since peewee league and my parents dragged me along to every game. I think I rebelled a little and decided from a young age that I just didn't care. Then he had to go pro and put my knowledge of the game to embarrassing shame."

"I'll teach you," he says.

"I don't want to learn," I fire back.

He laughs. "You're so...feisty. It's charming, hilarious, and hot all at the same time."

"Getting a little close to the line there, *friend*," I warn.

"Touché. My apologies. But I *will* impart some knowledge on you whether you like it or not."

"Fine," I challenge. "Then I'll teach you not to be such a cynical non-believer of fairy tales."

"So what do you do while the game's on, then?" he asks.

I laugh. "Usually I work. Now that I don't have a job, I'll probably read."

"Let me guess...something where they all live happily ever after?"

"Naturally," I say lightly. He's teasing me, but I refuse to be embarrassed for liking what I like.

My dad clinks a glass with a spoon to get everyone's attention. "Thank you all for being here this morning," he begins. "Josh and Nicole are ready to open their gifts. If you could all take your places, we can get started."

I glance at my plate. I've barely eaten anything, favoring instead the conversation with the hot guy sitting next to me. But maid of honor duties call.

Luke's shoveling in the sausage left on his plate, so I shovel in some eggs before I head over to Nicki. She hands me a pad of paper and a few pens. "Write what the gift is on the back of the card. The paper's for notes if you need to make any or if we can't find a card. And thank you."

"Of course. Happy to help." I repeat the words Luke texted to me last night after I thanked him for saving me in the pool. I sit back in the chair by my food, lonely now beside Luke's half-empty plate. He's talking to my mom in a corner of the room.

He comes back and sits to eat some more.

"What's your job here?" I ask.

"Help move the heavy stuff."

We watch as the happy couple tears the paper off wineglasses and kitchen utensils and picture frames. It's all the standard, cliché stuff they registered for even though they already have everything they could ever need due to my brother's healthy paychecks. But, according to Nicki's mom, everyone likes to bring a present to a wedding, so they still registered.

Once it's all over and my hand is stiff from writing every gift on the back of every card, it's time to check out of this hotel and the room where I was banged up against a window by Hot Luke.

And that means it's time to move in with my new roommate.

CHAPTER 15

The presents are split between five different cars, and we're all heading back toward Josh and Nicki's house to help unload before I move into Luke's place.

I still can't believe I'm doing this.

My heart thumps harder and faster with each present we unload. I'm getting nervous about actually moving in with him. Before, it was just this abstract idea set sometime in the future.

It's real now. And it's happening.

It's a temporary solution, but it's not like I'll move out in a few days. I don't even have a job yet. I haven't even *looked* for a job yet.

And it's not just all that making me nervous.

I recall him saying something about someone named *Pepper*. I'm still wondering who the hell that might be and whether the hell I'll get to meet her today.

Once everything is unloaded and we're standing in the driveway after saying goodbye to all the parents, who headed back to the hotel for a day of relaxing by the pool, Josh grins at me. "You ready to see your new place?"

I raise a brow, and Luke walks *literally* across the street and holds his arms out wide in a driveway that leads up to another stately mansion.

First things first. What the hell does a single guy need a house like *that* for? It's as big as my brother's.

And second, well, when Josh first told me his friend lived across the street from him, I sort of assumed he meant across a major cross street...not literally ten steps away. Not where he could look out his window and have a peek into Luke's place if the blinds are open.

"Wow, you weren't kidding about *across the street*," I say.

"Close enough to hear the construction on our renovations that'll surely start at the crack of dawn, but far enough that you won't be able to hear Nicki and me banging it out before we head to Fiji." Josh shoots me a smirk.

"Gross, Josh," I say, wrinkling my nose.

He grins and holds up his hands innocently. "Let's get you moved in."

It doesn't take much—just rolling my two suitcases across the street, really, which I could do by myself, but Josh and Luke each take one.

Luke opens the heavy wooden front door, and I hesitate on the front porch.

"You need anything else?" Josh asks beside me. Clearly he's anxious to get back to his new wife, who's probably already naked on their kitchen counter or something even more disgusting I don't want to think about.

I shake my head.

"All right, then. You two have fun, and if you need anything, I'll be busy across the street so find someone else to bother." He laughs and Luke flips him the bird just before he turns to walk away. He flips it back. "I love both of you," he says as he runs back across the street to his house.

"Come on in and I'll show you around," Luke says, but before he opens the door, we both hear a voice.

"Luke?"

It sounds like an elderly woman, and Luke faces the door and closes his eyes for a beat. He draws in a deep breath with his nose and exhales out his mouth before he turns around.

"Hey, Mrs. Adams," he says.

"Oh, Luke, you know I want you to call me Dorothy," a petite older woman with short white curls on her head and glasses perched on her nose says. She walks with a cane and moves just short of the bottom step of Luke's porch.

"Dorothy," he corrects himself. "How are you today?"

"Just stopping by to see who this pretty lady is and why she's walking into your house with suitcases."

I giggle. This woman is nosy, and she ain't shy about it. "I'm Ellie," I say.

Her eyes dart to me and seem to narrow a bit, like she's checking me out and judging whether I'm good enough to be in Luke's presence.

"She's Josh Nolan's sister and she's going to be staying with me a while," Luke says. "She's new to town and you better be nice to her."

"I'm nice to everybody!" she protests, and Luke laughs. "Why aren't you staying with Josh if he's your brother?"

I laugh. "They're doing some renovations." It's the simplest answer for a nosy neighbor, and it'll give her something new to spy on.

"What are your intentions with my Lukey?" she asks me.

I'd love to bang him into oblivion.

I don't say those words. Obviously.

"He's been generous enough to offer me a place to stay for a while. That's all," I say.

Dorothy raises a brow. "That better be all," she says, pointing her cane at me. "Because I'm the only lady allowed to sit on that lap."

My eyes widen and Luke coughs uncomfortably. "Okay, Mrs. Adams, we need to get inside. But we'll see you soon."

"Yes, dear. My granddaughter will be in town in a couple weeks and she'd love to see you again."

Luke shoots her a smile and nods, and then he rushes to unlock the door and open it.

"Nice meeting you," I say to Dorothy, and I wiggle my fingers.

"I'm not sure about that," she mutters, and Luke ushers me in and closes the door before she gets a chance to say more.

I step into a round grand entry, and this house is just as ridiculous as my brother's. A staircase with fancy iron railings sprawls in front of me, circling up to the second floor. When I look straight up, though, there's a circular skylight letting the sunshine into the entry, giving the effect of daylight inside. It's bright and white and not at all what I was expecting.

"So that's my neighbor, Dorothy Adams," he says.

"Yeah, I gathered that. She gets to sit on your lap?"

I swear his cheeks turn a little pink, and he shrugs. "She's always been a little, uh…openly flirtatious with me. She's always asking me to fix shit at her house or open a jar of pickles. Then she either moans or makes comments the entire time I'm working."

"Doesn't that make you uncomfortable?" I ask.

"Incredibly. But she's a little old lady with no family around, so I do what I can to help."

Aha! Another insight into Luke Dalton.

He's not a douchebag. He helps old women even though they're inappropriate with him.

Instead of harping on that point, I glance around at the entryway. "Why do you need such a ridiculously enormous house?"

He laughs. "I don't. Brutal honesty, my ex-wife picked it out. She was always much more into showing her status than I was, only a small part of why we're no longer together."

"And she didn't get to keep it?"

He raises his brows and shoots me a sly smile. "I'm here, aren't I?"

"Why haven't you moved?" I ask.

He hitches up a shoulder. "Mostly for convenience, to be honest. But also for the backyard." He points awkwardly. "So this is the staircase, and that's upstairs."

I giggle. It's about as stupid a statement as when I said *I'm the sister* earlier. "I figured. How many bedrooms are up there?"

He squints as he looks up. "Technically there's six, but I've converted a few of them. Follow me." We walk through the massive entry to a hallway that leads into the kitchen.

This isn't just a kitchen, though.

If I was a chef, this kitchen would be a freaking dream. Hell, it *is* a dream, and while I'm not a chef, I sort of know my way around the kitchen.

"Wow," I breathe as I look at the endless black quartz countertops with little sparkles in them and the white cabinets and the gray walls with a white subway tile backsplash. It's just so...massive. Imposing. Beautiful.

He points toward the room connected to the kitchen. "That's family room number one."

"Number one?" I ask, and he nods.

"I have two. Plus a massage room, a fitness room, a home theater, a study, two offices, a yard overlooking the mountains with a pool, a pool house that doubles as a weight and workout room, and some sports courts."

I stare at him with my jaw hanging open. I'm sure I look like an idiot, but this is where I'm *living*? No wonder why Josh said I wouldn't even have to see Luke. I probably *won't* with all this space.

"Sports courts?" I echo...never mind the freaking *massage room*. Does that come staffed? I'm not opposed to Luke just rubbing some oil on me.

He nods. "A full basketball court, a tennis court, and I had a customized field put in with turf so I could run drills in the off-season. The patio has some workout equipment, too. You're welcome to use anything. I have a small house staff. Sheila comes in Monday and Thursday to clean. Debbie comes by a few times a week to cook. Handyman Cam swings by once a week for pool maintenance and whatever else I need him for. So if you see these people around, they're all supposed to be here."

I follow him through the house as I try to gain my bearings. This is like a freaking orientation.

We stop in front of a closed door. "Ready for this?" he asks, and I shake my head as my eyes widen. I don't know exactly what I'm supposed to be preparing for.

He opens the door, and a wild beast lunges at him. Okay, maybe not a wild beast, but an adorably cute puppy who's very excited to see her owner.

Luke just laughs as the dog licks his arms, and then he says, "Pepper, sit."

Pepper.

Oh my God. Pepper wasn't some side chick at all! She's his freaking *dog*!

I feel a little better. I survey the room. It's the other family room, and it has a few couches and a television. Dog beds and toys are scattered around the room with a crate in the corner, dog bowls, and a doggie door that looks like it leads to a fenced side yard with grass. It's a dog's paradise, honestly.

"Ellie, I'd like to introduce you to Pepper, the current love of my life." He scratches her under her chin, and the dog sits patiently and wags her tail. "Do you like dogs?" he asks me.

I nod and kneel down. "How old is she?" She lunges for me, but Luke holds her back.

"Calm, Pepper," he says to the dog, and then he turns to me. "She's four months."

"And what kind is she?" I try to guess, but I'm at a loss. She's some kind of mix with multi-colored black, tan, and white fur, and she has blue eyes. She's possibly the cutest little thing I've ever seen…but she's actually not so little.

"A Goberian," he says, like I'm supposed to know what the hell that is.

"A Go-what now?"

"Golden Retriever mixed with a Siberian Husky. She could get up to ninety pounds, but she's supposed to have all the best traits from both breeds."

"How long have you had her?"

"Just picked her up a few weeks ago. Josh talked me into getting her." He laughs and shakes his head, like he's blaming my brother but actually isn't so mad about it. "And, incidentally, she's the reason I needed to jet out so quickly after our night together. My dog monitor app showed me she got out of her cage and this room was a damn disaster."

I blush as he brings up that night, and I wonder if I'll always feel a little embarrassed about it. It was a night that should've only left one impression, but neither of us had any idea that we'd meet again. Or that we'd end up as roommates less than seventy-two short hours after we met.

God, what a whirlwind three days it has been.

He shows me the sports courts and the outdoor living space and he takes me through the rest of the house. He leads me up the stairs, past some closed doors, and to the last room on the left. "This will be your room," he says.

He opens the door to a pristine and lavish guest room that overlooks the pool and the mountains. It has a huge bed with white sheets, a walk-in closet, and its own bathroom.

"Will this work?" he asks, and he almost seems a little...shy. Maybe even nervous. Like I'm judging his house.

"Will it work?" I repeat. I skip around the giant room and use one of the poles holding up the canopy over the bed to spin around—which probably makes me look like I'm a stripper rather than the whimsical look I'm going for. "Uh, hell yeah it'll work. How long did you say I could stay?"

He laughs, but before he can answer that, I chime back in.

"I'm kidding. I'm planning to start looking for a job tomorrow, and as soon as I get that squared away, then I'm hoping to find a place and get out of your hair ASAP."

"That's not necessary," he says softly, and his eyes burn from across the room by the door where he stands. "Take your time. It's a big house and most days it feels pretty empty."

Hence the reason for a dog, I'm guessing. Josh is definitely the meddling type who would make sure his friend didn't feel all alone in the gargantuan mansion across the street.

"You want something to eat?" he asks.

I nod, and then I follow him through the long hallway, down the marble and iron staircase, across the foyer, and finally to the kitchen. I note that he only showed me *my* bedroom. He didn't show me his or any of the others that had closed doors.

"Hey Pepper girl," he says to the dog, who's lying in the sun by the huge breakfast nook that's more like a dining room. "Let's see what Debbie left for us."

"Why'd you name her Pepper?" I ask.

"It's the leading lady in my favorite movie," he says.

My brows dip down. I can't think of any movies with Peppers in them.

"*Iron Man*," he clarifies. He rummages through the fridge and I pull out a stool on the other side of the counter from him and plop down. "We have bacon turkey ranch wraps or chicken salad sandwiches."

"Either. Can I help?"

He shakes his head and pulls out a container with the wraps in it. He grabs some plates and puts one in front of me and one in front of the spot next to me. "Drink?"

"Water is fine."

He grabs water, too, and then he sits next to me.

"So, Ellie, what kind of job are you looking for?" he asks.

"Public relations. Or, that was my field, anyway."

"What's the end-goal there?" He sips some water, and my eyes move to his lips as his tongue darts out to catch a drop.

An ache presses between my thighs.

I blow out a breath. "I mean, ultimately I would have loved to work my way up to higher profile celebrity clients."

"Well your roommate is a pro football player," he casually points out.

I roll my eyes. I suppose he wants free PR in exchange for offering me a room? I guess it's something I could offer, but certainly the team has a PR staff...right? "I mean *real* celebrities."

"Ouch," he says, patting his chest over his heart.

"You know what I mean," I say.

"Not really," he teases with an easy laugh. "Athletes aren't celebrities?"

My brother is an athlete. Is he a celebrity? I've never considered him one, but I guess the truth is that he *is* one. "I just mean like actors, musicians, that sort of thing. I don't know enough about sports to represent an athlete, though if the price was right, I'd learn."

"So money is what it'll take for you to learn football?" He raises a brow as he takes a bite of his wrap.

I lift a shoulder. "We all have our motivations, right?" Though when it comes to Luke Dalton, money is hardly the motivator. A quick flash of a smile would be enough for me to do just about anything.

And the more I think about it, the more interested I'm becoming in seeing him run around the field in those tight pants on Sunday afternoons.

Maybe I *am* suddenly interested in football.

"Speaking of which, I looked you up on social media and couldn't find you. Don't you have a PR manager or publicist?" I ask. I realize I just gave myself away, and that's my filter malfunctioning again, but I've embarrassed myself around this guy so much already that I feel like I can't really be any more mortified than I already have been.

He glances over at me with arched brows. "You looked me up?"

"Well, yeah. I had to know what I was getting into when I found out you were going to be my roommate." It's a lie. I totally looked him up because I couldn't stop thinking about him and I wanted to see his face again in a picture other than the one I memorized of us from the night of our hookup. "So why couldn't I find you?"

He lifts a shoulder. "I'm private."

"You can still be private and have social media."

He takes another bite of his wrap and lifts a shoulder. "I don't need it. I've gotten by fine for this long without it."

"So you're private, but you're willing to have a one-night stand with a random chick from a nightclub *and* you're willing to let your best friend's little sister live with you without ever having met her?"

He chuckles. "Those events are unrelated."

"Except they're the same person."

"Well, yeah, but..." he trails off. "I didn't know who you were that night, just like you didn't know who I was. It wasn't supposed to go past that one night, and I could tell you had no idea who I was, so that's why you ended up being the perfect candidate. Plus that sweet ass of yours."

I roll my eyes, but on the inside, butterflies batter around as my thighs clench together.

"And I trust Josh implicitly," he says. "I don't need to have met you to know you're trustworthy to stay here for a bit if you're cut from the same cloth as him."

I twist my lips, conceding. "Okay. But I'll get you to change your mind on social media."

"Then I'll get you to change your mind on football."

"Guess we've both got work to do," I say, and I take a bite of my wrap.

But the truth is...I don't mind one little bit being the *work* he has to *do*.

CHAPTER 16

Luke brought my suitcases up to the room that's mine and told me to make myself at home, and so I do.

I unpack, setting some clothes in the dresser and hanging others in the closet. I even unpack my toiletries, making the bathroom mine because it sure as hell beats living out of bags.

I toss the empty suitcases in the closet and move toward the window.

I sigh as I look out over the view of the mountains. I glance down at the yard. The sun shines down on the pool surrounded by palm trees, and this Chicago native *always* viewed palm trees as vacation.

But this is home now. For now, anyway.

Some movement near the patio catches my eye, and when I glance in that direction, my heart races and my brain basically malfunctions.

Luke.
No shirt.
Abs.
Sweat.
Muscles.
Running on a treadmill.
Focus and discipline and heat.
Drool. (That's me, not him.)
I blow out a breath.

So he's not a prince? Okay, maybe I can bend my fairy tale a little.

So he's already written me off? Okay, but if he can run on a treadmill right under my window without a shirt on, then...What?

I can walk in front of the window without a shirt on? Maybe.

Or I can come up with other ways to tempt him. I did, after all, already share a bed with him once, and we both admitted how hot it was. I'm not saying it has to be forever, but he was into me enough to give me one night.

But it was just one night. He didn't want more than that, and I still don't know why.

I get it—he's a private guy. But we're living together now, and I'm going to get to the bottom of this.

I force myself away from the window. I can't sit here and watch him all day or I'll go crazy.

I reorganize my makeup in the bathroom and then I head down to the family room. I toss my phone on the counter and head to the fridge for some more water. And then I look at the television. I see some remotes on an end table, and I pick one up.

I stare at it. I can't figure out which button is the power button, and I don't even know if the thing I'm holding in my hand is the right remote to turn on the television.

"Television on," I say, hoping that by some miracle that in the fanciness that is this house, technology will be on my side.

Nothing happens, but Pepper looks at me like I'm insane, her head tilted to the side and her ears perked up.

"Don't tell your daddy I just did that," I whisper to Pepper, and she just lets out a little whimper before resting her head on her paws.

I plop on the couch, and Pepper jumps up next to me. She settles onto the cushion beside me, turning in three circles before lying down with a heavy sigh, and I laugh at her even as I realize I have no idea if she's supposed to be up on the furniture. She looks so cozy, though, that I don't have the heart to make her get down. She settles her head on my thigh, and I stroke her soft fur.

Luke walks into the room through a door from outside that I honestly thought was just a big window. He's a little sweaty and he still isn't wearing a shirt. He chuckles when he sees me with his dog.

"You know," he says casually, "you're only the second woman who has met Pepper since I brought her home, but she did *not* like the first."

"Who was the first?" I ask.

"My ex-wife."

I giggle. "Sounds like you don't much like her, either."

He grabs a sports drink from the fridge and chugs a little of it down. "I don't," he says, and before I can dig a little deeper there, he offers a little more information. "We just don't share the same values."

"What does she value?"

"Money," he says, his answer firm and immediate. She seems like she scarred him a little.

"And you?" I ask.

"People. Hard work. Dedication. We were opposites in that way. She didn't care about the hard work it took to earn money, she just wanted to show off mine." He clears his throat, chugs some more of his drink, then lowers his voice a little. "What about you, Ellie? What do you value?"

"Well, I'd say work, but I don't have a job. But I did love what I used to do. I love when someone hands me a project and I get to take my creativity to solve a problem, so I guess I value creativity. I value my family, of course, and love."

"Fairy tales," he murmurs, and I chuckle. His phone rings, and he pulls it out of the band still attached to his arm. "Fuck," he mutters. "Speak of the devil."

He answers the call and heads out of the room, and he returns a few minutes later while I'm still petting (and conversing with) Pepper (who really hasn't given me any insights into her hot dad). He's freshly showered and sadly wearing a shirt.

He slides into a recliner across the room, and Pepper jumps down, leaps across the room, and jumps onto his lap.

"Traitor," I mutter.

Luke chuckles as he pets the dog. "I can't help that I'm her favorite human."

"We'll see about that. Just wait until she's fully grown and still leaping on you like that."

An easy silence passes between us, and then I ask, "So which remote actually turns the TV on? You didn't train me on those during orientation."

He laughs, and then he picks up Pepper and sets her on the floor. He stands, grabs all the remotes sitting there, and tells me what each one does—something I will never, ever remember, which I admit.

My phone starts to ring on the kitchen counter, and as I move to stand, he says, "I'll grab it for you."

"Thanks," I say as I juggle the remotes and set them down on the couch beside me.

He returns a few seconds later, and when he hands me my phone which he most certainly just saw, the image of the two of us that I snapped the night he left my hotel room shines brightly at me and he has a look on his face that clearly says he thinks I'm absolutely a crazy, insane stalker.

"Oh my God," I mutter in total mortification. Yep, that's right. I just told myself that I couldn't get embarrassed in front of this guy again because I'd already reached my limit, yet here we are again. "I swear to God, I put that picture on there as a joke before I even knew who you were. I was going to show it to Nicki and brag about my one-night stand and then I found out you were the best man and I just haven't changed it back yet."

I'm babbling and my phone is actually still ringing—it's a Chicago number I don't know but it has the same first three digits as my old office, so it's probably HR or something calling to tell me I won't get my last paycheck just to put the cherry on top of this shit sundae, and he's totally uncomfortable as he continues to look at me like I'm possibly dangerous.

I send the call to voicemail because I can't just answer a call when I need to fix this. I change the photo on my phone to the same picture I had on there before, which was just a pretty purple design, and then I flash my phone at him. "Better?"

"You're a little terrifying," he finally croaks.

"Yeah, I know."

He laughs, and then he sits back in the same chair which I will call *his chair*. Pepper jumps back on his lap. "So let's see...you stalked me on social media, you changed your phone wallpaper to a picture of us, and now you're living with me."

"Yep, that about sums it up." I twist my lips. "Okay, subject change. How's football going?"

"Well, we're in the offseason, so right now it's pretty stagnant. But the upcoming year is a contract year."

"What does that mean?" I ask stupidly.

"It means I have to play my ass off so my contract is renewed." He scratches Pepper behind the ears.

"How long do you want to keep playing?" I set my phone down next to me.

He lifts a shoulder as he keeps his eyes on the dog. "Forever? Football's just...everything to me. It's been a constant in my life since I was a little kid. I'm from a football family. My dad was a college coach and it was just sort of expected of me. It's all I ever wanted to do." His voice holds vulnerability that he hasn't shown me before. Apparently football is the thing that makes him emotive. I lean a bit in his direction as he opens up. "The Aces just drafted this kid right out of college, and that tells me they're looking at the future of the team. He's young and fast and he's going to slide right into my slot."

"You don't know that," I say, but maybe he does.

"I'm the oldest receiver on the team. The average age for receivers in the league is twenty-six. I'm thirty-one. The average career is two years. I've been playing for nine. It's only a matter of time." He doesn't seem at all like he's okay with that. In fact, that vulnerability has taken a turn to something else. A little bit of sadness mixed with some despondency.

"So what's your plan?" I ask, my public relations background forcing its way out. I'm not one to sit around and complain. I'm more likely to find the solution.

"To keep playing until I can't," he says.

"And then what?"

He twists his lips. "Nothing definitive."

"Broadcasting?" I ask.

He shrugs.

"Coaching?"

"Maybe."

"Okay, you need a plan, dude. You need something to look forward to. Isn't there something you've always wanted to do?" I ask.

"Yeah. Play football. I don't want to talk about what happens when I can't anymore."

Okay, so this guy is stubborn. I tap my chin and change the subject, but I don't forget about it. I just push it to the back of my mind for now. "Would you consider playing somewhere else?"

He shakes his head. "I've played for the Aces my entire career. I'd love to finish my career here, too."

"What if you were traded?" I ask.

He looks at me in horror. "We don't speak the 'T' word in this house," he says, and I think he's joking but I'm not totally sure.

"Then you make yourself essential," I say, as if the answer was obvious all along.

His brows push together. "How do I do that?"

"Simple," I say, suddenly feeling very comfortable in my own shoes. "We put together a PR strategy. And I know just the girl to do it."

CHAPTER 17

He rubs the back of his neck and tilts his head. "What sort of strategy?"

I shrug. "You already know I know nothing about football, but I know a little something about proving your worth. Off the top of my head, and I'm just thinking out loud here, but community outreach is a good first step. Charity work. Meeting fans, shaking hands, holding babies, that sort of thing. Becoming the fan favorite that brings money to the team will keep you around. Obviously you'll need to let people in via social media to do any of that."

He shakes his head and holds up his hands. "Nope. I'm out."

"Why?" I demand.

"Being a *fan favorite* won't secure my spot," he says.

"You don't know that."

"Uh, yeah, I do," he says. "I've been in this business a long time, and that's the thing, Ellie. It's a *business*. I'm just a pawn in the league's game, and there are thousands of men waiting to snatch my position away from me."

"But it couldn't hurt to step up your presence, could it?" I press, wondering why he's so against this. "Wouldn't that only help?"

"My *social media* presence? That's a hard no."

"Why are you so against social media?" I pry.

He glances away and doesn't answer.

"Look, you can still maintain your privacy. I'm just saying, post a picture of you and Josh from this weekend to show how your relationship translates off the field. It's not like you need to post my phone's wallpaper as you brag about your one-night stand conquest." My cheeks redden even as the words tumble out of my mouth.

Why, exactly, am I reminding him of this?

I press on. "A picture of your pool with your hand holding your Gatorade. No face."

"Then I look like I'm endorsing Gatorade," he says.

"Do you have a contract with Powerade?" I ask.

He shakes his head.

"Some other sports drink?"

He continues shaking his head.

"Then who cares? You like Gatorade, and you drink it after a workout. Cover the label if that makes you feel better. Post a picture of you working out on that treadmill on your patio. Post a picture of yourself playing basketball on your backyard court. You at practice. Your uniform. Hell, even a shot of your shoes for next season. It doesn't matter what it is. People want to feel like they have an inside pass to your life, and *that* is how you become a fan favorite. You want to be that guy that will cause a fan revolt if the 'T' word is even mentioned in this city."

He narrows his eyes at me. "Okay, well, for one thing, no, but for another thing, how would I even get any of those pictures to post?"

I give him a look like he's stupid.

I may be dumb when it comes to football, but clearly Luke is dumb when it comes to public relations.

"Uh, you have a roommate who's basically volunteering to help you, Luke. Social media is a key part of PR, and if you want me to be your expert, it'll be my job to curate your content, post it, and stimulate engagement." I pull my phone out and open Instagram. I search one of the clients I worked with back in Chicago and toss him my phone. "This is one of my former clients, and this is their Instagram feed. You can see the types of things I posted on their behalf."

"This looks great," he says as he scrolls through the photos and stops to glance at some of the captions. "But it's a restaurant. I'm an athlete."

I nod. "Yeah, those are two different things for sure, but the principles are the same. My job with the restaurant was to make it irresistible. I had to post pictures that made the food leap off the page. I had to show people having a great time. I had to make sure anyone scrolling would stop and feel the vibe I wanted them to feel. And those are the exact same things I'd do with you, but I'd use the word *indispensable* instead of *irresistible*."

I refrain from mentioning that he already *is* irresistible.

"I'd make people want to stop scrolling to get to know a piece of you that you've worked so damn hard to keep hidden. I'll make them feel the vibe that the Aces are nothing without Luke Dalton, and they won't continue to be a fan of the team if you're not on it. Their loyalties move with you, not with the team. Sort of like all these new Tampa Bay fans now that *you know who* moved," I say, speaking about one of the most famous quarterbacks in the league. I'm no expert but even I heard about that.

"By posting pictures of me on a treadmill?" He seems doubtful.

I smile. "Seems like you're starting to get it."

He's quiet as he mulls over my idea, and eventually he heaves out a long breath. "What if I agree to it?"

"Seriously?" I ask, my eyes wide in total shock at his complete one-eighty.

"Okay, forget it." He shakes his head and moves to stand.

"Wait!" I say, a little desperation there in my voice as I realize I need this job just as much as he needs me to do it. "If you agree to it, then I draft out a real plan, you approve it, and we get moving."

"What do you charge?" he asks.

For Luke Dalton? Nothing. The chance to get this insider view of his life? Priceless. "How about room and board?"

He chuckles. "Don't be ridiculous. You need a job, and you just pitched yourself to me. I wasn't looking to hire, yet you've somehow convinced me that I need you to keep my job. So I'll ask you again, and I mean apart from room and board since you'll have those here as long as you need them. What do you charge?"

I'm just supposed to come up with a number? I had a salary at my last job. I guess I could charge him a portion of what I took home every two weeks, but I had more than one client.

I also had a team of others behind me, including my ex. I won't have that here.

"Okay, how about this," he says to my silence as I weigh what the hell I should say. "I throw out a number, and you agree or disagree. Sound fair?"

"I need to draft your strategy first so you can determine what you think I'm worth," I point out.

"I think I know your worth," he murmurs, and I can't tell if he's flirting with me again or if he's accidentally dropping his thoughts aloud—sort of the same way I do sometimes. "But fine. Strategize and let's talk when you have it. How long do you need? A week or two?"

"I literally have nothing else going on. I can probably have it to you by morning."

He laughs. "Okay, roomie. Take the night off and work on it tomorrow. If you want, we could order something for dinner and just hang here with Pepper and maybe a movie. Sound okay? Good times with someone who's becoming a good friend."

My heart balloons during the part where he basically asks me on a date, but he manages to pop it just as quickly there at the end with his final word: *friend*.

That's all we are, and that's all he'll allow me to be.

For now.

I nod. "Sounds great. I've never seen the movie with Pepper's namesake, so maybe *Iron Man*."

He shoots me a look like I'm crazy. "You've never seen *Iron Man*?"

I shake my head.

"Then that's definitely what we're watching."

A few hours later, we're sprawled on the couch with Chinese food. Pepper lies on the floor by our feet with a chew toy, and the movie plays while we eat.

It feels like a date night in with my boyfriend.

But, I remind myself, that's not at all what it is.

In fact, depending what he thinks about the strategy I'm thinking about when I should be concentrating on the movie, it's sort of like a night in with my potential new boss.

CHAPTER 18

I stare down at the blank sheet of paper.

I swear, last night when we were watching that movie, I had about a million and one ideas for what to do, and now that I'm ready to draft the plan, I'm drawing a total blank.

It's not because Luke's out on the treadmill in his short runner's shorts and no shirt again. That's not what's distracting me except it totally is and my eyes keep moving toward the window because good God I could sit here and watch this show all damn day.

I make a list of food I want to keep around the house. Luke told me last night to add whatever I want to the general list and Debbie will pick it up. It's a great distraction when I'm supposed to be working.

It's quite the system here at Casa de Luke, and while I actually enjoy cooking, I'm certainly not the pro Debbie is. I basically add popcorn, extra bananas, and Smirnoff Seltzers (since Luke apparently only keeps beer and hard liquor around this place) to the list and call it a day.

"Focus, Ellie. Focus," I say aloud, and Pepper tilts her head at me in the same way she did yesterday, like she's trying to understand what I'm saying.

I draw in a breath, and then I pull up the worksheet I used to use at my old company whenever I'd draft a strategy. I immediately recall the acronym I always used when strategizing: SLUTS, or Situation assessment, Landscape trends, Usable data to help develop a plan, Timeline for the client, and, last, Setting goals.

He needs a lot of help. I'm going to start with social media, but he'll need a spokesperson who can handle interview, sponsorship, and collaboration requests, a publicist who can identify ways to get him out into the community, and a media relations specialist who can get the media to the same events he's at to ensure coverage. I'll need access to his agent and anyone else representing him. My specialty was always social media, but I have experience in the other areas, too.

When I think about assessing Luke's current situation and what he can do to change or improve...well, we're starting at zero. Literally. He doesn't even have an Instagram account, so anything we do will be an improvement.

I look at the landscape next. I search the top wide receivers, including my own brother, and study what types of things they post. I research other popular players and what makes them popular. I'll need more information there, and I write out all the questions I have for Luke as well as other areas to research so I can gather the most relevant usable data once I get the green light on this project.

I create a content calendar of what Luke will be posting for the next few weeks, but a lot depends on his schedule. I jot down some more questions for him. He admitted that football is his life, and when I look at what similar athletes are posting, I see a lot of collaborations and brand representing, lots of pictures of kids and families, pictures from professional events, and plenty of game day or practice action photos. I jot down a ton of notes, and I see what he means about taking a photo with a product because then he looks like he's repping that product. I'm sure once his page is verified as real, the offers will start pouring in.

And, finally, I set some goals. I note the average number of followers the most popular receivers have, which lands right around a million. And, most notably, our goal here is to make the fans fall even more in love with him by getting to know him so the entire organization will think twice about forcing him into an early retirement, though from what I've learned, his performance this season is the one thing that'll really prove he deserves to stick around. As much as I know he's attached to the Aces because it's the only place he has played, it's still a business, and if he doesn't perform to the level they need, well, they'll let him go.

All this from a few hours of research.

I glance over my plan, and I'm pretty proud of myself. I've never represented an athlete before, but if he agrees, this is going to look freaking amazing on my resume.

I bring my notes and questions to the kitchen, where I find Luke—or, rather, Luke's backside—rummaging through the fridge.

"I'm ready," I say.

He glances at the clock, surprise in his eyes when they return to me. "I figured you'd need all day."

I shrug. "I'm a fast worker, but also, I definitely have about ten thousand questions to ask you before I can finalize the strategy, so this is mostly preliminary and what I discovered through some quick research and data gathering."

"Okay," he says, pulling out a bag of baby carrots and popping one in his mouth. He crunches down on it. "Hit me with the plan."

I run through a quick presentation, sharing each part of my SLUTS acronym with him without actually calling it *SLUTS*, going over a few ways he can give back to the local community and build a brand for himself, and by the time I'm done, his brows are raised and he looks fairly impressed.

He nods. "Okay, I can get on board with building a brand. I like your community outreach ideas. And I can even approve photos of myself, or what I'm eating, or practice. Things like that. But my personal life is off-limits and my privacy remains intact no matter what."

"Of course. It's your social media even though I'm running it. I'll control it as much or as little as you're comfortable with," I say. "But can I ask why you're so worried about privacy?"

He stares at me for a beat as if he's weighing what to say, and then he doesn't really say anything at all. "It's just important to me. At the start, I'll need to approve everything, including captions and those stupid little number sign things."

"Hashtags?" I ask, and he nods. "Okay, micromanager."

He chuckles. "If you don't mind me asking, what were you making at your last position?"

"What is all this worth to you?" I ask rather than answering. "I'll tell you, but I'm just curious."

"Having you post for me a few times a week?"

"Daily," I say. "Not just to your Instagram profile page, but also to your stories. It's best to choose one platform to focus on, but I'll also get your Facebook and Twitter up and running. If you want Snapchat or Tik Tok, we can talk about that, too. I'll curate everything, maximize each post for your audience, and slowly build your engagement and your followers. But bear in mind that this isn't just me posting on your social media. I will sort of be your personal assistant when it comes to building your brand. I'll handle scheduling interviews, working on collaborations, and finding opportunities for you. So I'm not just your PR expert and your assistant since I'll need to basically run your calendar, but I'm also your spokesperson, social media manager, and publicist all for the price of one hot girl."

He laughs. "Definitely hot," he murmurs. "I've never had a personal assistant. I've never needed one."

"Do you think you need one now?" I ask. "Because you better believe it'll be my job to be up in your business all day every day."

He wrinkles his nose.

"I'll be in your face with a camera, and I'll expect you to be completely open and honest with me," I say. I lay it all on the line because what's the worst that can happen? He'll say no? Okay, then I'm right back to where I am now, and I'd rather be honest about what he can expect from me than surprise him later.

"I'm liking this idea less and less," he mutters. "But I want to stay with the Aces. I know I need to prove myself this season, as you mentioned, but none of this other stuff can hurt me. I have no idea what that's worth. Four hundred bucks a day, presuming you'll be working basically twenty-four-seven?"

My eyes widen at his number. That's, like, over a hundred grand a year. I try to mentally calculate it. Almost a hundred fifty.

Well over double what I was making before, but I wasn't *living* with my clients before, either. I didn't have any clients that were single entities that I had to brand.

Still...that's a lot of money, so I give him my honest answer. "That's more than double what I was making in Chicago."

He lifts a shoulder. "From your presentation here, I think you'll be well worth it. Let's try it for a week or two and see how we mesh, but I think we'll make a great team."

"Team Dalton," I say, and he laughs and holds up his knuckles.

I bump his knuckles with mine, and he agrees. "Team Dalton. Let's do this. Set me up on Instagram."

CHAPTER 19

A knock at the door pulls Luke's attention from my explanation of stories on Instagram, which, let's be honest, he was half-listening to anyway. It would be better if *he* took on the stories since I probably can't literally be with him every second of every day (even if I wish I could be), but it is what it is. Even better, I'd love to see him going live there or tossing up some video footage from practice or from charity events or whatever, but he has to actually listen to my training in order for any of that to happen.

"Excuse me," he says, and he heads toward the door. A few beats later, he yells, "Ellie! Your stuff's here!"

I jump down from the stool and head toward the door. A moving truck sits out front, and the excitement that my clothes and bullet journal supplies and blankets and shoes are all here rams into me. I came here with a couple of suitcases, but this...this is what makes a *home*.

"Where do you want this?" one of the men standing on the porch asks.

"Clothes and shoes in the bedroom, and anything else can go into one of my offices," Luke says. "We can move the rest from there."

"Are you sure?" I ask. "They can just put everything in my room."

He shakes his head. "It's fine. You don't want your room overflowing with boxes, do you?"

I shrug. I sort of figured that's how I'd live until I find a place of my own, but this works, too. I'll still have boxes overflowing *somewhere*—they'll just be out of sight.

"Thank you," I murmur, and the movers set to unloading boxes from the truck.

I left my furniture in my parents' basement just in case I decide to return to Chicago. I can find a furnished place out here, and once I decide whether I'm staying here permanently, we can figure out how to get my furniture here. Everything else I own is on the truck sitting at the curb.

"Bullet journal box one?" he reads off the side of one of the boxes stacked on the mover's hand truck. "How many bullet journal boxes are there, exactly?"

"Three," I admit with just a touch of embarrassment.

His brows dip. "Three?"

"Being creatively organized is *not* a crime," I say, and he just laughs.

My bullet journal boxes are stacked in his spare office, and my clothes and blankets and shoes are up in my room. I feel more at home with this stuff here even though I had the essentials with me. It only takes the movers about an hour to unload everything, and we head back to the counter to finish our Instagram training. I've only gotten about a minute into my explanation when the doorbell rings again.

Luke sighs and gets up to answer it. A few beats later, I hear him say, "What are you doing here?"

His voice sounds...tired. Weary. Annoyed.

I glance toward the direction of their voices, and if I lean back just a little, I can see his back from where I sit perched on a stool at the kitchen counter without making it totally obvious that I'm trying to spy.

It's just a totally different Luke than I've heard before.

"I just want to talk," the voice says, and it's a woman. "Can I come in?"

"No," he says. "If you want to talk, you can call or text me."

I lean back a little more in my stool to try to get a glimpse of the woman who's annoying Luke, but I lean a little *too* far back.

The stool topples backward with me still on it. I try to grab onto the counter to save myself, but I go right down with it. The fall toward the ground feels like it happens in slow motion, and it ends with a loud crash as my ass hits the floor at the same time as the stool.

"Oh, shit, Ellie!" Luke says from the front hall. He rushes back toward me to help me up, and my cheeks are absolutely *burning* with embarrassment as I stand. "Are you okay?" he asks. He picks up the stool and pushes it in at the counter.

"I'm fine," I mutter. Holy. Shit. I cannot believe I just did that. My ass took the brunt of it. I rub at it, and that's when he chuckles just a little.

Is he laughing? At me?

The woman he was talking to through the doorway rushes in behind him. She looks like she stepped off the pages of *Vogue* with her long, dark hair falling in a stick-straight curtain and dark eyes that are full of lust for Luke...and then there's me, the dork who just fell off a stool like some idiot.

Clearly Luke doesn't like her, made obvious by the way he told her she couldn't come in on top of the way he's looking at her like she should get the hell out of his house lest she stain something while she's inside it.

I'm glad he's never looked at me with that sort of wrath, but remind me to stay on his good side.

Is this the ex-wife? The ex-girlfriend? The ex-*something*?

"Who is this?" she demands, plopping her purse down on the counter.

"I'm Ellie," I say stupidly. I think of all the ways I can identify myself. His best friend's sister? His roommate? His one-night stand? His...

"My fiancée," Luke supplies.

Wait.

What?

That definitely wasn't one of the words I just thought of.

My eyes meet his. The way they silently beg tells me that I need to agree to this.

I need to fake this with him in this moment, and he can explain later.

And so I do what I've wanted to do every second I've spent with him.

No...not that. There's a woman watching us with her mouth hanging open just a tad in complete and utter disbelief, so I can't do *that*.

I lace my arm around his waist and press a kiss to his cheek.

The stubble there is rough under my lips, transporting me back to a hotel room on the Strip, and I'm so close that I feel his heat against me. He smells familiar with that fresh, manly scent that I memorized in those few beats where we collapsed on the bed together and I breathed him in.

Our night flashes back to me. It's almost painful how much detail flashes back.

Being so close to him...it's just the slightest hint that makes me crave so much more. An aching pulse throbs between my legs, and I am royally screwed.

I want my brother's best friend who just told some woman we're engaged even though he vowed that I'm off-limits to him.

And I want him *bad*.

He tosses his arm around my shoulders, and I flex my fingers where they're wrapped around his torso. Good God, I feel a little dizzy this close to him. Focus, Ellie. Focus.

"Your fiancée?" the woman repeats. Her disbelieving voice matches the expression on her face.

"Yeah," Luke says. He pulls me in closer.

"Weren't you not even dating someone like five minutes ago?" she asks snidely.

"It's actually none of your business. So what did you want to talk about?"

His fingers dig into my shoulder, and clearly this woman makes him tense. I'm sure I could find ways to relax him...

"She isn't wearing a ring," she accuses, her eyes flashing to my left hand.

"She doesn't need one to proclaim her status to the world like some people I know," he retorts.

Yes! Go Luke.

"Well whatever," she says, clearly trying to pretend like this doesn't throw her for a total loop.

"Why are you here?" Luke asks.

"Aren't you going to introduce us?" she asks slyly, ignoring his question and acting like she already has a game plan for overcoming the wrench in her plan that is me.

I stay as quiet as I can while Luke handles this situation however he wants to. I'm just along for the ride at this point.

"Ellie, it's my sincerest regret to have to introduce you to my ex-girlfriend, Michelle."

"Oh, I'm more than his ex-*girlfriend*," she says snidely, like she hates the very word. "We were lovers. We were connected in every way two humans can be connected."

Luke rolls his eyes. "And yet we're not anymore."

"I've heard so much about you," I lie smoothly, giving her my fakest, most sugary smile as I stick out my hand to shake hers.

She doesn't return the handshake, so I'm just standing there with my hand out like an idiot.

So, rather than feel like an idiot, I turn to Luke and ask, "Is she the coffee spoon in the sugar bowl girl?"

He barks out a laugh, and my chest is positively *glowing* from making him laugh like that.

She narrows her eyes at me. "I've heard nothing about you. She's not your usual type, Luke." With those words, she spins on her heel and heads toward the door, both of us following her. "Looks like I've got a big story for Savannah, so you should let me know when you can fit me into your very busy schedule." She presses her lips together in a fake, tight smile.

"Oh, fuck you, Michelle. Expect a call from my lawyer."

"I'll be looking forward to it." She winks at me, unruffled by this entire exchange—or at least pretending like she is. "His lawyer is a hottie, am I right?" She wiggles her fingers and says, "Ta-ta for now." She sashays out the front door like she still lives here.

Luke slams it closed behind her, and he sighs deeply as he stands there facing it. When he turns back toward me, I'm wide-eyed and silent as I look at the weary expression on his handsome face. I may not know him all that well, but clearly this woman does things to him that both age and exhaust him. I'm inclined to give him a hug, but we definitely aren't at that stage of our friendship yet.

Even though I'm apparently engaged to him.

"I'm sorry," he mutters.

"For what?"

He glances over at me. "For using you in my lie." He balls his fists. "For telling her you're my fiancée. I shouldn't have put you in that spot. She just makes me so goddamn angry that it just slipped out."

I clear my throat. I have a lot of questions, but there's one that's sort of pounding in my chest with every beat of my heart. "Who's Savannah?"

He draws in a long breath, and his eyes meet mine for a beat before he answers. "My ex-wife. Michelle's apparent new best friend...and a journalist."

CHAPTER 20

"Well, I think I get why you're so private now."

He chuckles mirthlessly, and then he walks through the house and collapses on the couch like the entire encounter with Michelle took more out of him than his morning runs on the treadmill. He draws in a heavy breath. "Savannah is technically a sports reporter, but she found fame reporting on the personal lives of athletes. I was not exempt from that during our marriage, and that's a big reason why we're no longer married. Well, that and she's an insufferable nightmare."

I laugh as I sit a cushion and a half away from him. "Tell me how you really feel. What did she publish that got your panties all twisted up?"

He glances at me for a beat before he leans back and stares up at the ceiling in contemplation, like he isn't sure how much to tell me. And then, maybe because he trusts me, maybe because he's paying me for publicity, or maybe because I've made a fool of myself hundreds of times in the short period of time we've known each other, he spills some tea.

"She asked me if she could write what she called a tell-all series of articles based on my brother and me."

"You have a brother?" I ask.

He nods. "Jack Dalton. Current starting quarterback for the Broncos, but he's also played in Dallas and San Diego, back when the team actually *was* in San Diego. On his way to the Hall of Fame. God, you really don't watch football."

I laugh and hold up a hand. "Sorry. So what did these articles say?"

"I didn't love the idea, but I wanted her to find success in her career. And she did. Those articles *made* her career. The first few were great, but then she started to paint this rivalry between us. And there *was* always a rivalry there, but she made it worse. It became less of a sports report and more of a tabloid exposé."

"That's awful," I murmur, even though I'm insanely curious to find those articles. "So why is Michelle running to her?"

He rolls his eyes. "Attention. Plus I'm sure Savannah will pay her for the gossip, and tomorrow our engagement will be everywhere."

"Is that why you threatened her with your lawyer?" I ask.

He nods, and then he shrugs. "It's useless, though. That type of journalism isn't illegal, even though it should be. Unethical, yes, but not illegal."

"Well that sucks. So why'd you tell her we're engaged if you knew she'd run to Savannah?"

"I don't know," he mutters. "It just slipped out before I even gave it a second thought. I wanted to hit her with something I knew would hurt her because she hurt me, too." He glances over at me and shoots me a wry smile. "See? I told you. I'm no prince."

I let that last comment slip past. "So am I supposed to pretend we're engaged?"

He rubs the back of his neck. "Maybe?" He tilts his head as he thinks it over, and he shakes his head resolutely. "No. Your brother would *kill* me."

"Why not? Would it help get her off your back?"

"I can't ask you to do that," he says. "I shouldn't have said what I said. I put you in an awkward position, and I'm sorry."

"Why can't you ask me to do that?" I ask, genuinely curious.

His brows dip down. "You're young and single and gorgeous. You could have any guy who's looking for a relationship, and I can't be the guy who holds you back from finding that. Not when it's not what I want."

I roll my eyes, but it doesn't escape me that he just called me *gorgeous*.

"What?" he asks.

"Dude, I'm not looking." I laugh. "Let me spell it out for you. I just got out of a thing, I'm brand new to Vegas, I'm trying to figure out my job situation with my roommate boss. I'm handling enough shit right now, so trust me when I say that hunting for a boyfriend isn't a priority for me at the moment."

"But what about your brother? And how long will you fake this with me?" he asks. "Eventually you'll want to move on."

And by that point, I'll have Luke so in love with me that it'll all just magically fall into place for us.

Right?

Yeah, I doubt it, too.

"We can cross that bridge when we get to it," I say instead. "And we'll explain everything to Josh. If he knows it's fake, he won't get mad. Right? Besides, he married my best friend. Why can't I marry his?"

He sighs. "I don't know, Ellie..."

I reach over and give his forearm a gentle squeeze, ignoring the way just touching his skin with mine lights a fire in my belly. "I saw how awful she was," I say. "You're giving me a place to stay and you're giving me a job. I want to help you, too."

He presses his lips together as he thinks about it, and then he nods.

"Okay," he says. "Let's fake it." He twists his lips, crinkles his nose, and shrugs, and it's about the cutest thing I've ever seen. I laugh, and we're both quiet for a beat.

And then I ask softly, "What did she do to hurt you?"

"Aside from the coffee spoon in the sugar bowl?" he quips, and I smirk.

"Yes, aside from that."

"She's just...not a nice person. She said things that dug deep when we broke up."

"Okay, so then we're definitely engaged." My brows draw down. "Were you ever engaged to her?"

He shakes his head. "She begged me for a ring. *Begged*. I can't even admit some of the things she tried to get me to commit. But I held strong."

"Because you knew she wasn't right for you?"

He sits up and shakes his head. "No. Because I don't plan to ever get married again."

I feel like I'm getting whiplash here. "But you said we're engaged...and being engaged usually leads to a wedding..." I'm trailing off my sentences as I try to put the pieces together.

"Right. It's fake, Ellie. Remember?"

I nod even though I feel a little deflated.

Wait.

I feel...*deflated?*

Because he just reminded me that he told his ex a lie about being engaged to me?

In what world should that *deflate* me?

"So what's the next step, then? A fake wedding?"

His brows dip down a beat, and I wish I knew him well enough to read those facial expressions, but I don't. Not yet, anyway.

"Your brother would kill me on that one, so no. If we get married, it has to be real."

My eyes widen. "What?"

He laughs. "I'm kidding. I already told you, I'm not getting married again."

Right. And I'm the one who wants the happily ever after with my Prince Charming. More reasons he isn't right for me...and yet every little piece of him I'm getting to know makes me want to learn more.

This is starting to go deeper than a simple attraction or the lust of wanting him on top of me naked again.

I'm starting to genuinely like this guy, and that's a real problem considering he's not interested. Even though he did just tell his ex-girlfriend that I'm his fiancée.

"So...I'm confused. Do you really want to play that we're engaged or what?"

He shrugs. "Well, yeah. In front of her, at least."

"So what happens when she blabs to Savannah?"

"That's an extra bonus since that's another woman who's always trying to squeeze more money out of me." He sighs. "I guess we're doing this."

He really hasn't had a lot of luck finding a nice lady.

Enter Ellie.

CHAPTER 21

When I wake up the next morning, I check my email just like I always do.

And my mouth drops the fuck open. All the way to the floor.

I was expecting the story to hit...but I was *not* expecting *this*.

I rush down to the kitchen. It's empty.

I dart around the first family room, where I find Pepper on the couch, who just looks at me like I'm an idiot (like she always does), and then I look out the window.

Sure enough, there's Luke running on the treadmill on the patio.

No shirt.

I realize I haven't even looked in a mirror yet after rolling out of bed and I prefer to look my best particularly when I'm about to see the object of my crush...but the news on my phone is more pressing than how I look right now.

It's more pressing than what he's doing.

I run outside and wave my phone at him. He's concentrating and focused as he runs, and it takes him a beat to even notice I'm standing there. Once he does, he slows to a jog and slips out his earbuds as his brows dip down.

I wish I could just take a minute to stare at the perfection that is the man on the treadmill.

Okay, I do it even though I have something important to say. I stare shamelessly, my eyes flicking to his abs and to his legs and back to his handsome face. He's sweaty and I don't even care because he's freaking gorgeous. I lament the fact that I'm the one who has to break this news to him since he has no clue as he runs without a care in the world on his treadmill.

"Ellie, what's wrong?" he asks. His eyes are wide. Clearly I've frightened the man with my freshly just rolled out of bed look.

"She ran to the media," I say, more out of breath from running through the house looking for him for the last sixty seconds than he is from running on a treadmill for probably the last hour.

His eyes flick to my chest covered by the flimsy white material of the tank top I slept in. I'm not wearing a bra. It's bright out here. I'm dying of embarrassment as I realize he can probably see my nipples. Why didn't I think to at least change my shirt? Maybe run a brush through my hair?

Oh, right.

Because of the headlines that cluttered my inbox this morning.

He narrows his eyes at me, but he slows his jog to a walk, and eventually he shuts the thing off and steps down. He grabs a towel and wipes the sweat from his face then slings it around his neck.

"You have to see the headlines." I hesitate for a second since I don't want to be the one breaking this news to him, and then I hand him my phone.

He glances at the headline.

Aces Receiver Luke Dalton Set to Wed Amidst Baby Scandal

And the byline? Savannah Buck.

He looks back up at me, but his expression is unreadable. He has to feel *some* way about that headline. "How did you find this?"

"I set up an alert so any time an article is published about you, it goes to my email. And before you get any crazy ideas that I'm some kind of stalker, it's a standard part of being a public relations manager."

He heaves out a breath, and I wish he was more forthcoming with what he's thinking. He's schooled himself to hide his emotions, and he does a good job of it. I just haven't figured out *why* he does it. But I will.

"Well, alright then," he says. "Looks like the news is out. We're engaged."

"And the rest of the headline?" I prod.

"Shit like this gets printed all the time." He shrugs like he's blowing it off.

"Luke, there's only *one person* in the entire world who thinks we're engaged." I'm trying to impress upon him that this is more serious than he realizes. My gut tells me this isn't some joke. This is his ex. She was here yesterday saying she needed to talk to him, and he blew her off, and she ran to the press with her news since he didn't take the time to listen. "Just read the article."

He scans it. Michelle didn't just run to Savannah to let her know Luke is engaged. Michelle also ran to Savannah to let her know that she's pregnant.

With Luke's baby.

To be continued in Book 2, **LONG GAME**.

ACKNOWLEDGMENTS

Thank you to my husband for everything you do. The support, encouragement, and love is what makes this possible. Thank you to my kids for nap time and quiet time when mommy gets to write, and thank you to my parents who love hanging out with my babies so I can get some computer time in.

Thank you to Trenda London from It's Your Story Content Editing, Diane Holtry and Alissa Riker for beta reading, Najla Qamber for the gorgeous cover design, and Katie Harder-Schauer from Proofreading by Katie.

Thank you to Wildfire Marketing, my ARC team, Team LS, and all the bloggers who read, post, and review.

Thank you to you, the reader, for taking time out of your life to spend it with Ellie. I hope you enjoyed what you read, and I can't wait for you to read the next book.

xoxo,
Lisa Suzanne

ABOUT THE AUTHOR

Lisa Suzanne is a romance author who resides in Arizona with her husband and two kids. She's a former high school English teacher and college composition instructor. When she's not cuddling or chasing her kids, she can be found working on her latest book or watching reruns of *Friends*.

ALSO BY LISA SUZANNE

A LITTLE LIKE DESTINY
A Little Like Destiny Book One
#1 Bestselling Rock Star Romance

TAKE MY HEART
My Favorite Band Book One
#1 Bestselling Rock Star Romance

Printed in Great Britain
by Amazon